WITHDRAWN

Introduction to
SOCIOLOGY

Bruce J. Cohen, Ph.D.
C. W. Post Center
Long Island University

Terri L. Orbuch, Ph.D.
University of Iowa

W9-CNB-032

An American BookWorks Corporation Project

McGraw-Hill Publishing Company

New York St. Louis San Francisco Auckland Bogotá Caracas Hamburg
Lisbon London Madrid Mexico Milan Montreal New Delhi Oklahoma City
Paris San Juan São Paulo Singapore Sydney Tokyo Toronto

MADISON-JEFFERSON COUNTY PUBLIC LIBRARY

About the authors

Bruce J. Cohen received his doctoral degree from Michigan State University in 1964. He was on the faculty and served as an administrator at Michigan State before joining the faculty at the C. W. Post Center of Long Island University in 1970 as full professor. From 1970 to 1973 he served as Chairman of the Department of Sociology at C. W. Post and in 1973 he was appointed Chairman of the Department of Criminal Justice. He returned to the faculty in 1985.

Terri L. Orbuch received her Ph.D. in sociology from the University of Wisconsin-Madison in 1988. She is currently a post-doctoral fellow and visiting professor in the department of psychology at the University of Iowa. She has written numerous articles and book chapters on relationship loss, human sexuality, and aging/lifecourse development.

Introduction to Sociology

Adapted from *Schaum's Outline of Theory and Problems of Introduction to Sociology*. Copyright © 1979 by McGraw Hill, Inc. All Rights Reserved.

Copyright © 1990 by McGraw-Hill, Inc. All rights reserved. Printed in the United States of America. Except as permitted under the Copyright Act of 1976, no part of this publication may be reproduced or distributed in any form or by an means, or stored in a data base or retrieval system, without the prior written permission of the publisher.

1 2 3 4 5 6 7 8 9 10 11 12 13 14 15 16 17 18 19 20 FGR FGR 8 9 2 1 0 9

ISBN 0-07-011597-4

Library of Congress Cataloging-in-Publication Data
    Cohen, Bruce J.
       Introduction to sociology / Bruce Cohen, Terri Orbuch.
       p. cm. — (McGraw-Hill college review books series)
       "An American BookWorks Corporation project."
       ISBN 0-07-011597-4
       1. Sociology.   I. Orbuch, Terri.   II. Title.   III. Series.
    HM51.C584 1988
    301—dc19   90-13235

301
COH

Preface

Sociology is the systematic study of the group life of human beings. Although it is the youngest of the social sciences, it encompasses fundamental principles that, once recognized, illuminate the course of human social history and offer profound insights into the diverse social problems of today. As a unifying approach to many aspects of the human condition, sociology has proved to be a valuable course of study not only for those who major in it but also for students of history, political science, economics, business, psychology, and anthropology.

This volume presents an overview of sociology, with emphasis on its basic concepts and theoretical perspectives. Designed to accompany any of the standard textbooks and to supplement classroom instruction, it can also serve as a concise text. Its clear and logical organization of topics makes it ideal for both initial study and review. A glossary provides definitions of key terms, terms that may be unfamiliar, and terms that have a special meaning in sociology.

Bruce J. Cohen
Terri L. Orbuch

Contents

Part   I: What is Sociology? 1

CHAPTER 1
Introduction to Sociology 3

CHAPTER 2
Sociological Research 11

Part   II: The Individual and Society 27

CHAPTER 3
Culture 29

CHAPTER 4
Socialization and the Self 37

CHAPTER 5
Sexuality and Gender Roles 47

CHAPTER 6
Deviance and Social Control 57

Part III: Social Organization 73

CHAPTER 7
Social Groups 75

CHAPTER 8
Social Institutions and Formal Organizations 84

CHAPTER 9
Marriage and the Family 99

Part IV: Social Stratification 117

CHAPTER 10
Social Class and Social Mobility 119

CHAPTER 11
Race and Ethnic Relations 131

Part V: Change 141

CHAPTER 12
Social and Cultural Change 143

CHAPTER 13
Population, Ecology, and Urbanization 152

CHAPTER 14
Collective Behavior and Social Movements 163

Glossary 181

Index 195

Part I:
What is Sociology?

Sociology has been defined as the systematic study of the development, structure, interaction, and collective behavior of organized groups of human beings. However, it is much more than the definition implies. The insights that sociological research provides give us a way of looking at ourselves as social beings that illuminates every aspect of our lives.

The following two chapters introduce the field of sociology. Chapter 1 sets forth its scope, its historical development, and its relationship with other social sciences. Chapter 2 explains the different techniques by which sociologists collect their data, how they validate research results, and the ethical considerations they must always take into account.

CHAPTER 1

Introduction to Sociology

Individuals live a good deal of their lives in groups: they interact with each other as the members of a family; as residents of a neighborhood or town; as members of a particular social, economic, religious, and/or ethnic group; and as the citizens of a nation. Even when people are not conscious of themselves as members of a group, they think and act in ways that are at least in part determined by group membership. The types of clothes they wear, how and what they eat, the beliefs and values they hold, and the customs they follow are all influenced by their membership in various groups.

Sociologists are interested in the group life of human beings. They examine the patterns and arrangements of societies, the processes through which they develop and change, and the interplay between these patterns and processes in the behavior of individuals and groups. A sociologist may have strong feelings or beliefs about how society ought to organize itself or treat certain of its members, but it is not these feelings or beliefs that define this person as a sociologist. A sociologist, as a professional, is obliged to report on and analyze objectively the nature and structure of societies.

This chapter provides a general introduction to the field of sociology. It sets forth the reasons sociology is an important scientific study, discusses the relationship between sociology and the other social sciences, and traces sociology's historical development.

The Study of Sociology

Sociology may be defined as the scientific study of human interaction. It is concerned with the way in which individuals interact as members of groups and institutions, both individually and collectively, and how these interactions are connected to the larger culture and social structure of a society.

The study of sociology is important for many different reasons.

1. Through sociology, we are able to take a fresh look at the social environment and to reexamine our place in society along with groups and cultures with which we seldom or never have contact or about which we previously knew little or nothing.

2. By understanding the origin of viewpoints and attitudes that are quite different from our own, we may ultimately understand the social forces that influence our own behavior and the behavior of those around us.

3. The study of sociology may help to alleviate prejudices and stereotypes and make us more flexible in adapting to novel situations.

4. By analyzing the nature of society, particularly the institutions and groups within societies and the effect of these organized processes and patterns on group living, the field of sociology provides us with new ways of looking at and reacting to the ever-changing face of social reality.

The insights of sociologists have been of great value to educators, community planners, medical workers, government officials, and businesses. Sociological information on past social trends and their causes can help policy makers plan for and shape the future. For example, in order to provide adequate services for the American people, our government must be able to predict what conditions will exist in future years and identify needs that must be met. Social planners, using the findings of sociologists, are able to forecast future needs for schools, medical facilities, correctional institutions, and retirement centers, to name just a few.

Sociology and Other Sciences

The sciences are customarily divided into two major branches: the natural sciences and the social sciences. The natural sciences are concerned with physical phenomena, the social sciences with the broad spectrum of human behavior. Sociology is a social science.

Other social sciences include political science, the study of government, political philosophy, and administrative decision-making; economics, the study of the production, distribution, and consumption of goods and services in a society; and anthropology, including archaeology (the study of the remains of extinct civilizations), linguistics (the study of language), physical anthropology (the study of human evolution), and cultural or social anthropology (the study of the ways of life among communities throughout the world).

The disciplines of sociology and cultural and social anthropology share many common concepts. Psychology and social psychology are often confused with sociology. Psychology is the study of individual behavior and processes. Social psychology is the study of an individual's relationship with a group. Social psychologists may have a sociological orientation and focus on social behavior as a product of the interaction between individuals and groups, or they may have a psychological orientation and focus on social behavior as a product of intrapsychic processes. Geography (the study of the features of the earth and their effect on the growth, decline, and movement of world populations) and history (the recording and explanation of past human activities) are also related to sociology.

Sociology as a Science

Like the other social sciences, sociology is less rigorous than the natural sciences. There are two basic reasons for this. First, the scientific method has only recently been applied to the study of social behavior. Second, dealing with human subjects presents many problems that are absent in the natural sciences. Individuals change behavior in ways that may significantly affect their relationships with one another and with the scientists who wish to study them. Nevertheless, sociology as it is pursued today is based on observed, verifiable evidence. The sociologist's methods of gathering data, making observations, and stating generalizations relating to the data are based on scientific procedures.

Sociology uses the scientific method in its attempt to find answers to important questions. In this method of inquiry the following conditions must be adhered to:

1. *Verifiable Evidence*. Scientific inquiry requires concrete and factual observations that can be checked for accuracy. Since verifiable evidence is essential to scientific investigation, the studies of various metaphysical problems, such as the existence of God or an afterlife, are eliminated.

2. *Rejection of Absolutes*. Science admits no absolute truths. Scientists must always be prepared to examine new evidence; therefore, scientific truth must remain tentative.

3. *Ethical Neutrality*. Science may answer questions of fact but cannot prove that one value is better than another. Science seeks knowledge, but society's values ultimately determine how this knowledge is to be used. The scientist acting as an individual is not ethically neutral but nevertheless, must not let personal values influence the design and conduct of professional research.

4. *Objectivity*. The sociologist must have a detached and impersonal view of the matter under consideration. All observations must be recorded in unbiased terms, and stereotypes must be avoided.

5. *Standardized and Stringent Study Methods*. The sociologist must use accurate and correct descriptions of the data under investigation. Furthermore, there must be an organized plan for collecting data, and upon the collection of data, all procedures and findings should accurately be recorded.

6. *Professionalism*. It is imperative that scientific observations be made by well-trained observers, for the untrained observer may

misinterpret what has been seen. In evaluating reported observations, the sociologist will want to know the degree of special knowledge or training the observer has received.

Do common sense and intuition have a place in sociology? Yes, for they often contribute to the development of hypotheses. In and of themselves, however, common sense and intuition are not sufficient as techniques for sociological research.

The Scientific Method of Investigation

Sociological investigations, like all scientific investigations, should proceed through the following steps on the way to a conclusion:

1. *Formulation of a Hypothesis.* After a problem is identified, a theoretical statement relating all known facts is made. Scientific hypotheses are statements that can be tested and either confirmed or disconfirmed with empirical evidence.

2. *Research Design.* In planning the research design, the sociologist outlines what is to be studied, collected, processed, and analyzed, then chooses a research method (see Chapter 2) by which to collect the data.

3. *Collection of Data.* All necessary data are collected in accordance with the above-stated research design.

4. *Analysis of Data.* Scientific analysis requires that the data collected be classified and tabulated, and all necessary comparisons be made.

5. *Conclusion.* After the above steps have carefully been followed, the sociologist determines whether the original hypothesis was confirmed or disconfirmed, or if the results were found to be inconclusive.

Historical Development of Sociology

Sociology, the youngest of the social sciences, nevertheless has a historical development of its own. The questions about society posed by the early theorists have not only played an important role in the development of sociological thought but also continue to influence it.

Auguste Comte. The word "sociology" was first coined in 1838 by Auguste Comte, a Frenchman, in his work *Positive Philosophy.* Comte is generally referred to as the father of sociology. He believed that the science of sociology should be based on systematic observation and classification, the same principles that governed the study of the natural sciences.

Herbert Spencer. In 1876, Herbert Spencer, an Englishman, developed a theory of "social evolution" that, after being accepted and then rejected, is now being accepted once again in modified form. Spencer applied Darwin's theory of evolution to human societies. He believed that there exists a gradual evolution of society from the primitive to the industrial. In his writings he indicated that this was a natural evolutionary process that should not be interfered with by humans.

Karl Marx. Karl Marx (1818–1883) was also an important figure in the development of sociology. He proposed that all societies are made up of two basic classes that are in constant opposition: those who own or control the means of production, and those who don't. Fundamental to this viewpoint is the assumption that those who own the means of production use this power to exploit and oppress those who do not. The social behavior of individuals is determined by their position in the class society.

Lester Ward. In 1883, Lester Ward, an American, published *Dynamic Sociology.* In this work he advocated social progress through social action guided by sociologists.

Emile Durkheim. In 1895, Emile Durkheim published *Rules of Sociological Method,* outlining the methodology used in his classical study of suicide in various population groups. Durkheim, a pioneer in the development of sociology, firmly believed that societies were bound together by the commonly shared beliefs and values of their members.

Max Weber. Max Weber (1864–1920) believed that the methods used in the natural sciences could not be applied to the problems explored in the social sciences. He argued that because social scientists study the social world in which they live, there must be a certain degree of subjective understanding in their investigations. He believed that in their work, sociologists should be value free, never allowing personal biases to influence either their research or their conclusions.

Courses in sociology were offered at many universities in the 1890s. In 1895, the *American Journal of Sociology* began publishing, and in 1905 the American Sociological Society—now called the American Sociological Association (ASA)—was founded. Currently, most sociologists are members of the American Sociological Association and gather at the association's annual meetings in order to address, discuss, and debate new research in the discipline.

Specialized Fields in Sociology

The discipline of sociology is divided into a number of specialized fields, some of which are listed below. A sociology department at a university or college may offer classes in each of these fields of study. Most of these topics are reflected in the chapter titles of this book.

Applied Sociology

Collective Behavior and Social Movements

Community

Criminology and Delinquency

Cultural Sociology

Demography

Deviant Behavior

Environmental Sociology

Human Ecology

Industrial Sociology

Marxist Sociology

Marriage and the Family

Medical Sociology

Methodology and Statistics

Political Sociology

Race/Ethnic/Minority Relations

Rural Sociology

Social Control

Social Organization

Social Psychology

Social Stratification

Sociology of Aging

Sociology of Education

Sociology of Emotions

Sociology of Sex and Gender

Sociology of Occupations and Professions

Sociology of Religion

Theoretical Sociology

Urban Sociology

CHAPTER 2

Sociological Research

All sociological research makes use of the scientific method, but the specific techniques of data collection and analysis differ from one sociological study to another. There are four general techniques: the case study, the experiment, the observational study, and the survey. Time factors are extremely important; sociological studies may be cross-sectional, longitudinal, retrospective, or prospective. Statistics are used to analyze data collected.

Special issues are involved in sociological research: those inherent in the techniques employed and those arising from ethical considerations and constantly changing social conditions. This chapter provides an appreciation of the kinds of choices sociologists must make when they develop research projects, the complexities of actually doing research, and the skepticism with which one should approach conclusions drawn from sociological studies.

Research Techniques

There are many techniques by which sociologists collect data in order to make generalizations about the social environment. The four

11

techniques most commonly used in sociological research are the case study, the experiment, the observational study, and the survey. These research techniques are not mutually exclusive alternatives, but rather different angles from which a researcher can approach a research question. The goal of the study, pragmatic concerns, and the researcher's theoretical perspective usually determine which of the above techniques, or combination of the techniques, is used in research.

Reliability and Validity

In deciding which technique(s) to use, the techniques are often evaluated in terms of the reliability and validity of the data collected.

Reliability is defined as the extent to which the same research method will produce the same results each time the method is employed. High reliability is preferred and is a key index of just how well a study was conducted.

There are two types of validity. *Internal validity* refers to the extent to which the data obtained actually reflect the real condition(s) being investigated. In order to obtain high validity, the results of the research study must accurately reflect the conditions of the subject(s) under investigation. *External validity* refers to the extent to which the results from the subject(s) in the present study can be generalized to individual(s) not presently under investigation.

Just as each of these research techniques provides sociologists with certain tools, so each has certain requirements and presents particular problems. These issues and the four research techniques are discussed in the following sections.

Case Studies

The case study is used by sociologists to make a detailed account of some phenomenon. A researcher conducting a case study collects a vast amount of detailed and rich information from a small number of subjects under study. For example, in a case study, data may be collected: (1) from a small group of child molesters, in order to obtain an abundance of information on the individual characteristics of these criminals; (2) from a social organization such as the United States Army in order to obtain detailed information regarding its specific rules and regulations of hiring; or (3) on a social movement such as the gay and lesbian rights movement, in which the focus is on the social structural elements, the cultural framework, and the interpersonal processes that occur within that social movement.

If the case study deals with events that have already taken place, the investigator will carefully research records pertaining to the event and interview available persons who were either directly or indirectly involved. For example, if a sociologist wished to investigate a religious cult that flourished twenty years ago in a small rural town, the researcher would probably want to visit the town and interview anyone old enough to remember the cult in question. In addition, the researcher would want to examine any written evidence, including town records, old newspaper accounts, and correspondence, that may shed some light on the cult and the people who were in it.

Strengths and Weaknesses of Case Studies

The main advantage of the case study is that it gathers rich data on a phenomenon without limiting the data collection to asking questions or interviewing subjects. A researcher is able to make reliable statements about a particular event, organization, or group of people, using detailed data. The reliability of the data collected in the case study is high.

The main disadvantage of the case study arises when a researcher wants to generalize beyond that particular event, organization, or group of people. The case study has limited external validity because the researcher is never sure if another group of subjects, organization, or event will behave in the same manner as the group, organization, or event currently being examined. Furthermore, the size of the sample in the case study is usually small, which limits generalization of the data beyond the present study.

Experiments

In an experiment, all variables but one (the independent variable) are held constant (or controlled), and the sociologist records what happens as he/she manipulates the independent variable.

Variables

A variable is anything that varies from one situation to the next. For example, individuals may vary in socioeconomic status, gender, age, and religiosity; organizations may vary in power, cohesiveness, and complexity; events or situations may vary by historical period, political orientation, number of people in a situation, and ambiguity in defining the situation.

Any variable can be either an independent variable or a dependent variable, depending on the nature of the particular study.

An *independent variable* is defined as the variable that is manipulated within the experiment. The researcher usually has some hypothesis about how the independent variable will affect the outcome of the experiment.

A *dependent variable* is defined as the outcome variable; the variable that a researcher is interested in measuring and about which he/she would like to make conclusions.

While experiments usually take place in a laboratory setting, they may be conducted in the field if the experimenters are able to hold constant all but the independent variable. This means that in any particular experiment only the independent variable, which is manipulated by the experimenter, is purposely varied as the study moves from one experimental trial to the next.

Control Groups

In order to see if and how changes in the independent variable affect the dependent variable in the experiment, a sociologist would divide the subjects into a control group and at least one experimental group. The purpose of the control group is to establish a basis for comparison. The people in the control group are subjected to the experimental situation, and then their responses are compared with the responses of the subjects in the experimental group(s), where the independent variable has been manipulated in some other way. The sociologist, by comparing the responses of the groups, can then come to a significant conclusion about the effect of manipulating the independent variable.

For example, if a sociologist wanted to examine the effect of audiovisual aids on the performance of students in an undergraduate economics course, he/she would design an experiment that contained a control group and at least one experimental group. The independent variable would be labeled as the use of audiovisual aids and would be manipulated in the experiment. The performance of students in an undergraduate economics course is the outcome variable that the researcher is interested in examining and would be labeled the dependent variable. The control group would receive a series of fifty-minute lectures in which the teacher makes extensive use of a blackboard to sketch simple graphs, charts, and so on. The students in the experimental group would receive the identical series of lectures, but audiovisual aids (such as slides and film strips) would replace the teacher's blackboard sketches. By testing the performance of the two student groups at the end of the lecture series (the dependent variable), the sociologist could come to some tentative conclusions about the effect of the audiovisual aids on the learning process.

The sociologist in this example would want to make sure that it was the presence or absence of the audiovisual aids and not some other factor that influenced the outcome. To make sure that this is the case, the sociologist would want the people in the control group and the people in the experimental group to be substantially alike. The only significant difference between them would be that one did and one did not encounter the audiovisual supplements.

Sociologists select and set up control and experimental groups in basically two ways. In the first, called the *matched-pair technique,* the experimenter sees to it that for each person in the control group there is a corresponding "matched" subject in each of the experimental groups. (Subjects who are "matched" are like each other in terms of certain crucial variables.) In the second technique, called the *random-assignment technique*, the subjects are placed in either the control group or in one of the experimental groups according to a statistically random assignment.

Strengths and Weaknesses of Experimental Studies

The major strengths of the experimental study are that (1) the researcher has complete control of the independent variables in the study, and (2) the researcher can rule out the influence of other confounding factors that may influence the results by using the matched-pair or random-assignment techniques. The data obtained in an experimental method have high reliability because of these two strengths.

The primary weakness of the experimental method is that its results may not apply to events outside of the experimental setting. The real world may not be as controlled (or constant) as the experiment, and therefore the results have limited or unknown validity.

Observational Studies

Like experiments, observational studies can take place either in the field or in a laboratory setting. Observational studies differ from experiments, however, in that the sociologist does not manipulate an independent variable in order to test its effect on the subjects. Instead, the researcher attempts to record his/her systematic observations of an actual (rather than an arranged) situation. The phenomenon under investigation is usually ongoing interaction in groups or settings.

Observation Methods

The researchers in an observational study may or may not interact directly with the subjects of the study, depending on what effect the designer of the study thinks observer participation or nonparticipation will have.

Participant Observation Method. In the participant observation method, a researcher participates in the group or setting that is being studied. Oftentimes the researcher must participate in order to be accepted by the group under investigation and thereby gain information about the group's behavior. For example, if a team of sociologists wishes to conduct an observational study of a small town in rural Wisconsin over a twelve-month period, the researchers may move into the town, becoming full-time residents for the duration of the study. In becoming participants of the group under investigation, researchers gain more information about the behavior of the residents.

Nonparticipant Observation Method. The main disadvantage of the participant observation method is that the researchers may develop a bias to an event because they participate in it. When researchers are concerned about this bias, and feel that by interacting in the event they may somehow affect the event itself, researchers use the nonparticipant observation method. In the nonparticipant observation method, a researcher observes a group or setting without interacting or participating in the phenomenon under investigation. For example, a sociologist who wished to observe the interactions of a group of kindergarten children might do so by viewing them through a one-way mirror in a specially equipped schoolroom. It is also important to point out, however, that in the nonparticipant observation method, data collected may be biased by the mere fact that an event is being observed, especially if subjects know that they are being observed.

Strengths and Weaknesses of Observational Studies

The main advantage of observational studies is that researchers are able to obtain detailed information about ongoing behaviors without interrupting or manipulating the behaviors. The researcher is examining a group or setting as it naturally unfolds.

The major weakness of the observational method is that a researcher, not having complete control over the event being examined, may not be able to generalize any results beyond the specific event under investigation. For example, the team of sociologists examining the rural town in Wisconsin may not be able to generalize their findings beyond the specific town they observed. There may exist special properties of the town they observe that are not present in other rural towns. Furthermore, the observational technique must take extraordinary care in training the individuals who are recording the event. All observers must have the same criteria in mind in order for the results to be reliable.

Survey Studies

If a sociologist identifies a specific group (or population) and wishes to make a generalized statement about the beliefs, values, and attitudes of its members, the sociologist can do so by using the observational technique and observing or questioning each member. However, if the researcher wishes to examine the beliefs, values, or attitudes of an identified group that is extremely large (for example, if the population is defined as American males 65 years of age and older), it is not feasible to interview or even observe every member of this population.

The survey method is therefore used by sociologists who want to make statements regarding large groups (or populations) of individuals. The data are gathered, usually through questionnaires or interviews, from a portion of the identified group or population. These data are then used to make generalized statements about the total group (or population). The survey method obtains information on the *incidence* (how many) of a specific phenomenon and the *frequency* (how often) with which the phenomenon occurs in an identified group (or population).

Data-Gathering Techniques

In order to collect the necessary information, one of two data-gathering techniques, the interview or the questionnaire, is generally used.

Questionnaires. Questionnaires are either directly handed to subjects to fill out or mailed to subjects. The manner in which the questions are worded and ordered often affects the reliability of the data obtained from questionnaires.

Interviews. In the interview technique, the researcher asks the subject questions face-to-face or over the telephone. Either a structured or an unstructured interview may be conducted.

In the *structured interview*, each respondent is asked the same set of questions in precisely the same order. Although this type of interview is inflexible, the data obtained may easily be tabulated and compared. For example, if the sociologist wishes to study voting patterns among different social-economic groups, the following question might be used in a structured interview:

Question: What statement most accurately describes your voting habits?

I rarely or never vote 1

I usually vote only in presidential elections 2

I usually vote only in important local elections . . 3

I usually vote in both national and local elections . 4

The *unstructured interview* provides much more flexibility for the researcher and freedom of response for the subject. Questions may be explained in more detail, and follow-up on significant responses is often encouraged. Unlike the structured interview, the unstructured interview often results in responses that are very difficult to compare. In the study on voting patterns among different social-economic groups, the unstructured interview might take the form of a dialogue, as follows:

Question: When do you usually vote?

Response: I have voted in the school budget elections for the past 20 years.

Question: Do you also vote in political elections?

Response: Yes, I vote in the state election for governor every four years. That is the only political election I participate in.

As can be seen, while the intent of the researcher may have been to elicit similar information in both the structured and unstructured interviews, the information actually elicited from subjects would be somewhat different in the two types of interviews.

Types of Samples

The extent to which the sociologist can make generalized statements about a particular group of people is dependent on the type of sample selected for study. There are three main types of samples: the convenience sample, the volunteer sample, and the random sample.

The Convenience Sample. The convenience sample contains individuals who are conveniently available to the researcher. The individuals are not selected because they possess any prior characteristic. Studies that attempt to make generalizations to the total population using data obtained from college students or persons on the street rely on convenience samples. Because these samples may not be representative of the larger population, results obtained from convenience samples have unknown external validity.

The Volunteer Sample. The volunteer sample consists of individuals who have volunteered to participate in a study. For example, magazine readers are often asked to answer questionnaires and return them to the magazine. The magazine then reports the results of their survey. Results based on this type of sample also have low external validity, because subjects who volunteer to participate may possess a certain characteristic that can affect the results of the study. For example, research reports that individuals who volunteer to answer magazine surveys are more liberal on social issues.

The Random Sample. If a sociologist wishes to make generalized statements about a particular group of people, those selected for study from the group must represent the larger group or must possess the general characteristics of the group as a whole. The preferred type of sample in a survey study is the random sample. Data obtained from random samples have high external validity. The sample of individuals is chosen from the group or population at large using special random techniques that assure that every individual in the identified group or population has an equally likely chance of being selected into the sample.

Strengths and Weaknesses of Survey Studies

The major strength of survey studies is that they can obtain incidence and frequency information on a large group of individuals. The data can be reliable if the researcher is attentive to question formatting and wording. The degree to which the data have high external validity depends on the type of sample used in the study.

The major weakness of the survey method is the fact that only limited information can be obtained from the subjects in the study. Rich and detailed data, which can be obtained through the case study method or the observational method, are beyond the reach of the survey method.

Time Factors Involved in Research

All research is carried out within some specific time reference. Time-related studies can be cross-sectional, longitudinal, retrospective, or prospective.

Cross-Sectional Studies

The cross-sectional study is a comparison of situations existing among different groups at the same point in time. If a sociologist wishes to study the factors that influence married couples either to stay together or to divorce, he/she might obtain a sample of divorced couples and a sample of married couples and then compare the groups on certain relevant factors. This study would be an example of a cross-sectional study because it examines two groups at the same point in time.

Longitudinal Studies

The longitudinal study is an investigation of one subject or group carried out over a long period of time. If a sociologist wishes to design a longitudinal study investigating why married couples either stay together or get divorced, he/she would obtain a sample of married couples and follow the couples for an extended period of time (such as two years). At the end of the designated time period, the sociologist would then compare what factors are present in those couples who divorced and what factors are present in those couples who stayed together.

Ex Post Facto or Retrospective Studies

An ex post facto or retrospective study is an effort to research a situation that occurred at an earlier point in time. For example, if a sociologist wished to study adolescent birth control practices, he/she might investigate this behavior by asking a group of sexually active adolescents whether they had used birth control during their first inter- course experience.

Prospective Studies

A prospective study is one that begins with the present and is extended into the future for a certain period of time. This is a very costly method of research when the length of the time of the study increases. For example, if the sociologist studying adolescent birth control prac- tices wanted to design a prospective study, he/she might obtain a sample of sexually inactive 13-year-olds and collect questionnaire data on their attitudes and behaviors regarding birth control. This sociologist would study these adolescents until they became sexually active, then attempt to determine which prior attitudes and behaviors did or did not influence some adolescents to use birth control when they became sexually active.

Use of Statistics

Sociologists rely on statistics to state the facts about what is occurring in the data they have collected. The following statistical definitions are basic to sociological statistics; these are the statistics most commonly used by sociologists to analyze their data.

The Mean

The mean is the arithmetic average obtained by dividing the total of all the cases by the number of individual cases involved. For example, assume that the following test scores were received by nine students taking a course in Introduction to Sociology: 50, 60, 80, 57, 66, 90, 60, 78, 99. The mean score is 71 and is obtained by adding all the above scores and dividing by nine.

The Median

The median is the number that falls midway in the distribution of numbers. The median score in the above example of test scores is 66. Four scores are above the test score of 66, and four scores are below the test score of 66.

The Mode

The mode is the number that appears most often in the distribution. In the above example the mode is a test score of 60.

The Range

The range is the interval containing all the numbers from lowest to highest. The range of test scores in the above example is 50-99.

The Coefficient of Correlation

The coefficient of correlation measures the relationship between two or more sets of variables. Coefficients of correlation run from −1.00 to +1.00.

When a perfect positive relationship exists between two variables, the coefficient will be +1.00. Any positive coefficient of correlation signifies that a change in one variable (increase or decrease) is associated with the same type of change (increase or decrease) in the second variable. For example, if years of education and occupational status are correlated at +.89, this signifies that an increase (or decrease) in years of education is associated with an increase (or decrease) in occupational status.

When no relationship exists between two variables, the coefficient will be 0.00.

When a perfect negative relationship exists between two variables, the coefficient is −1.00. Any negative coefficient of correlation signifies that a change in one variable (increase or decrease) is associated with the opposite type of change in the second variable (decrease or increase). For example, if hours of exercise per week and weight gain are correlated at −.89, this signifies that an increase in the number of hours an individual exercises is associated with a decrease in weight gain (or weight loss).

Special Issues in Sociological Research

Because the sociologist is dealing with human subjects and with varying lifestyles, personalities, values, and traditions, he/she encounters research problems that are often very different from those faced by the natural scientist.

Changing Conditions

The sociologist must be aware of the continuous modification of social conditions, which necessitates time and space qualifications in all reports. Although changes occur in the physical sciences, the degree of change within relatively short periods of time may be much more dramatic within the social sciences. For example, planning, coordinating, and conducting sociological research is usually a time-consuming process. If one wanted to keep tabs on what types of crime were most prevalent in a community so that preventive measures might be implemented, a study that would last one year might be undertaken. After data collection, analysis, and review of the findings, authorities may discover that the incidence of a particular kind of offense has diminished and new crime problems have emerged.

The sociologist must also be aware that the very fact of studying social behavior has an effect upon it, sometimes changing it radically. The natural scientist must also be aware of this effect, but the impact is less relevant for a scientist who is studying atoms in a test tube or elements in an astronomical universe.

Ethical Considerations

Unlike the natural and physical sciences, sociology has great limitations placed on it regarding what kinds of research are ethically and morally acceptable. A sociologist deals with human subjects and must respect their rights, wishes, and dignity. Many of the research projects conducted at universities, governmental agencies, and foundations must go through a Human Subjects Committee or Board that decides whether the research is acceptable.

There are four ethical considerations that researchers must address when designing a research study. All participants of a sociological study should be aware of the following:

The Nature of the Study

Individuals who participate in a research study must obtain a fair description of what the study will consist of. Researchers do not need to explain why they are conducting the research and what their hypotheses are regarding the study; however, they need to inform the subjects what will be done to them.

The Risks and Benefits

Subjects need to be informed of the risks and benefits to them if they participate in the study. For example, if a large contraceptive manufacturer tests a new birth control method on a sample of women, the women should be informed if this method of birth control is suspected of having any harmful side effects. The subjects then have the option of participating or not in the study.

Confidentiality

Subjects need to be assured of confidentiality. Information should not leak out that might match a name of a specific subject to his/her responses or behaviors. Survey studies therefore often use only code numbers to identify respondents.

Voluntary Participation

Subjects should recognize that their participation in the study is voluntary. After reading or hearing the description of the study and the risks/benefits to them should they participate in it, subjects need to be informed that they have the right not to participate, and to withdraw their participation at any time during the study.

Roles of the Sociologist

Certain questions concerning propriety emerge when one considers the proper role of the sociologist. At times the sociologist acts as a scientist, at other times he/she is a participant in society. The following four roles represent the most important roles of the sociologist. These roles are not mutually exclusive, and as is frequently the case, a sociologist can play several of these roles concurrently.

Research Scientist

The sociologist can be a research scientist. In this role, the sociologist conducts scientific research and in so doing, collects and organizes knowledge about social life. Nearly all research sociologists are employed by universities, governmental agencies, foundations, or corporations. At a university, the sociologist may be engaged in teaching and research (funded or unfunded) concurrently.

Policy Consultant

The sociologist can be a policy consultant. In this role, the sociologist predicts the probable effects of a social policy. Many social policies have failed because they were not scientifically researched but were based on unsound assumptions and predictions.

Technician

The sociologist can be a technician. Many sociologists are employed by various corporations, governmental agencies, and so on in order to make the organization more efficient. In this kind of work, the sociologist must especially be careful not to place the goals of the organization above the ethics of the profession.

Teacher

The sociologist can be a teacher. Teaching continues to be the major career of most sociologists. As a teacher, the sociologist is in a position to exert a tremendous influence over his/her students. A sociologist who teaches must always be aware of the ethical issue of possible indoctrination of students by encouraging a particular course of social action.

Part II:
The Individual and Society

Although sociology may seem to emphasize groups, institutions, and organizations, it does not lose sight of the individual. Individuals together form societies and develop cultures; in turn they are shaped by the societies to which they belong and the cultures they share.

The next four chapters examine the relationship between the individual and society. Chapter 3 discusses culture—what it encompasses, how it is organized, and how it is communicated. Chapter 4 looks at socialization, the process by which individuals acquire the values and norms of their culture and develop a sense of self. Chapter 5 considers the part society and culture play in the development of one's sexuality. Chapter 6 turns to deviant behavior—the failure of individuals to conform to the norms and expectations of society—and the mechanisms society sets up to control it.

CHAPTER 3

Culture

Social behavior varies from society to society. Interacting with others, human beings learn appropriate social behavior and the meanings of these behaviors in their society. It is these learned behaviors and shared meanings—the culture of a society—that ensure human cooperation and survival. This chapter takes a broad look at culture: the forms it takes, how it is acquired and transmitted, and how it may change over time.

Culture as Distinct from Society

The words "culture" and "society" have distinct but related meanings. Sociology defines culture as the sum total of the learned behavioral traits, values, beliefs, language, laws, and technology characteristic of the members of a particular society. The key word in the above definition is *learned,* which distinguishes culture from behavior that is the result of biological inheritance. All newborn infants cry when they are hungry or in discomfort. This type of crying, a behavioral trait observed in all human societies, is not a distinguishing trait of any particular culture; rather, it is an unlearned part of a human's biological inheritance.

A society, on the other hand, is a group of people who live together over an extended period, occupy a territory, and eventually begin to organize themselves into a social unit distinct from other groups. The members of a society also share a culture. It is impossible for a culture and a society to exist apart from each other. If there exists a society, there must be a corresponding culture. The United States, like other societies, has a culture that has been handed down from one generation to the next. Included in this culture are technology, religious institutions, language, values, beliefs, laws, and traditions. This culture has been transmitted by both formal agents of socialization (e.g., schools, religion) and informal agents of socialization (e.g., peer groups, media).

Symbolic Communication

The one factor that truly sets humans apart from animals is their ability to communicate at a sophisticated level. The highly developed human faculty for symbolic communication facilitates the acquisition of culture and makes possible the transmittal of culture between generations. Sociologists and anthropologists agree that if humans did not have the ability to develop language and communicate, they would not have survived as a species.

Humans communicate with symbols in three basic ways: spoken language, written language, and nonverbal behavior.

Spoken Language

Spoken language is patterns of sounds with meanings attached to each. Spoken language facilitates teaching and communication.

Written Language

Written language is the graphic recording of spoken language. It facilitates the preservation of learning and the legacy of culture. Remedies to aid the sick, agricultural techniques, blueprints for housing, and methods of construction of tools have all been recorded. Each generation can contribute to its society's culture by studying and building on what has been done in the past.

Nonverbal Behavior

Nonverbal behavior is the exchange of meanings through nonlinguistic elements of vocal behaviors, gestures, and body postures. There are three types of nonverbal communication: *paralanguage* (vocal behaviors such as pitch or loudness of speech), *kinesics* (body movements such as hand movements or facial expressions), and *proxemics* (interpersonal spacing or body postures). All of these nonverbal behaviors are learned and connote different meanings in different cultures.

Cultural Norms

A cultural norm is an established standard of what a group expects (or approves of) in terms of thought and conduct. These expectations and resultant behaviors often vary from one culture to the next. A cultural norm differs from a statistical norm. A statistical norm is defined by empirical data and represents behavior that actually occurs. These statistical norms are facts rather than matters of opinion. A cultural norm, on the other hand, represents an expectation about what behavior should exist.

Cultural norms take many different forms, including values, folkways, mores, and laws.

Values

Values are the deep-seated sentiments or perspectives shared by members of a society that will often dictate the actions and behavior of its members. For example, American society puts a high value on family life, individual liberties, the free press, and equality before the law. These values are subject to interpretation, but they are widely and deeply held in our society.

Folkways

Folkways are the customary, habitual ways of acting within a society. Examples of folkways shared in the United States are eating hot dogs at a baseball game, wearing formal attire at a wedding, and driving on the right-hand side of the road.

Mores

Mores are customs carrying significant implications of right and wrong. The mores of a society are often incorporated into its legal system and religious teachings. Mores may change through both an unconscious, unplanned, and nondirected process, or by enacted change that is planned and deliberate. In the United States, there are strict prohibitions against murder, assault, treason, rape, and incest. In addition to these rather obvious mores, there are many others that attract strong public reaction if violated, such as the contemptuous use of religious symbols and appearing naked in a public place.

Laws

Laws are mores of particular significance that have been formalized into rules. In order to reinforce the mores of a society, it is sometimes necessary to enact laws. Those who break these rules are faced with the threat of legal punishment. Even though murder, rape, and robbery are forbidden by our system of mores, some members of society will not respect these mores even if they are formally threatened with punishment sanctioned by law.

The Organization of Culture

A culture is organized in a systematic manner, permitting individuals and groups to interact efficiently.

Cultural Traits

A cultural trait is the smallest unit of a culture; it may be a phrase, an object, a gesture, or a symbol. The bats, balls, gloves, uniforms, and all the other material objects used in a baseball game are cultural traits, as are the particular gestures, rules, and terminology specific to the game.

Cultural Complexes and Institutions

A cultural complex is a cluster of related traits. An institution is made up of several cultural complexes focusing on an important activity or function. As an organized and patterned system of social relationships, an institution permits functions to be performed and individual and group needs to be met. The sport of baseball is a cultural complex made up of specific related traits, and this complex is itself a part of the larger organized system of social relationships known as the recreational institution.

In order to carry out necessary functions and meet the needs of group members, all societies have maintained five basic social institutions: the familial, educational, political, economic, and religious institutions. Other institutions have evolved in modern societies, for example, the military and recreational institutions in the United States.

Subcultures

Society can also be divided according to subcultures; groups of people who share cultural complexes, but that are smaller than a society. Each subculture is related to the larger culture in the sense that it accepts many of its norms, but the subculture is also distinguishable because it has some norms of its own. All members of the dominant culture are also members of specific subcultures (e.g., ethnic, religious, and class subcultures).

Countercultures

Countercultures are made up of groups (subcultures) that sharply challenge and reject some of the norms and expectations of the dominant culture. The delinquent subculture has often been used as an example of a counterculture in American society. The values, as defined by middle-class society, of hard work, self-discipline, and high aspirations are rejected by members of the delinquent subculture. Although the delinquent subculture rejects some of the values of the dominant culture, it accepts others such as competitiveness and survival of the fittest. The members of the subculture are not isolated from the larger society, for they come into contact with traditional middle-class institutions in many ways. Furthermore, countercultures do not necessarily have a negative impact on the dominant culture; they often instigate social change, and some social change is beneficial.

Integrated Cultures

If a culture is to function efficiently and serve the needs of society, its various elements must work together properly. Cultural integration is the functional, integrated organization and operation of all traits and complexes in a culture. An integrated culture is one in which cultural traits and complexes are tightly interrelated; a change in one complex is likely to cause a change in another, and a change in the culture at large.

The Functionalist Perspective

The term "cultural integration" implies that society consists of many related parts which combine to form a connected and organized whole that meets the needs of most of its members. This viewpoint is a functionalist perspective of society. All parts of society perform certain functions for the needs of a stable and consensual society.

The Conflict Perspective

Sociologists who espouse the conflict perspective do not agree with this view of society. Conflict theorists view society as organized according to the needs and values of those individuals in power. These values and needs are then imposed on individuals with less power, which creates conflicts of interest between different groups and classes within society. According to the conflict perspective, the consensus of needs and values that the functionalist perspective posits is not a true consensus of society. Moreover, culture may not be as integrated and interrelated as the functionalist theorist presumes.

Ethnocentrism

Ethnocentrism refers to the tendency of individuals in a society to assume the superiority of their own culture. We are often encouraged by inculcated societal attitudes to be ethnocentric, because of both habit and tradition. Thus, when members of a group judge nonmembers, ethnocentrism often leads to a feeling of superiority. Even though all groups stimulate the growth of ethnocentrism, all members of the group are not equally ethnocentric. Certain types of personalities tend to be more ethnocentric than others.

There are many examples of ethnocentrism. People who live in cities view country folks as "hicks," while the country folks in turn view urban dwellers as "city slickers." Young people are unwilling to accept the "establishment," while adults look down upon what they consider to be rebellious, inconsiderate kids. Christian missionaries see members of an underdeveloped tribal society as a group of heathens, while the members of that underdeveloped society look at the missionaries as strange people with weird objects that they idolize.

From the standpoint of society, ethnocentrism has both beneficial and detrimental effects. Ethnocentrism reinforces group loyalty and heightens the level of morale, patriotism, and nationalism. It also serves as a protection against change by advocating preservation of a culture within society. On the other hand, ethnocentrism inhibits change or innovations that have beneficial consequences for a society. For example, a problem within a society that may easily be solved through social change may unfortunately remain if outside ideas are looked upon with suspicion and are considered wrong. In its extreme form, ethnocentrism leads to a needless rejection of the wisdom and knowledge of other cultures, erecting barriers that prevent cultural exchange and enrichment.

Cultural Relativity

It is impossible to understand the behavioral patterns of other groups if we analyze the behaviors only in terms of our own cultural motives and values. Cultural relativism signifies that the meaning and value of a cultural trait should be judged in relation to its cultural context. The value or function of a cultural trait is not inherent in the trait itself, but is defined according to the culture wherein the trait resides. A trait that is disruptive in one society may be vital to the stability of another. The value of a custom in a culture can only be judged by the contribution it makes to its culture.

For example, athletes engaged in some professional sports have become more and more aggressive in their play. In a sport such as ice hockey, to fight with players of the opposing team has taken on positive connotations of hustle, hard play, and aggressiveness. It is not uncommon for players to be seriously injured by meeting the expectations placed on them during the game. For outsiders viewing professional ice hockey, it is sometimes impossible to understand this behavior in the light of values that place importance upon human life and nonaggressive behaviors.

Cultural Change and Cultural Lag

All cultures experience some degree of change over time, although people are reluctant to relinquish old traditions, values, an ' customs in favor of new ones. The methods and the rate of change will of course vary. Cultural change occurs whenever new traits and trait complexes appear in a culture and thus alter the culture's content and structure.

Change is more likely to occur in the material culture. Technology (part of the material culture) is perhaps the most important agent for producing cultural change. While people are likely to accept changes in technology, they are less likely to modify their norms, values, beliefs, or social organization (nonmaterial elements of culture). The result of such a disparity is a cultural lag. In other words, when the material elements of culture change faster than the relevant nonmaterial elements, a lag develops: in an evolving society, the nonmaterial elements in time catch up and keep pace with changes in the material elements.

For example, suppose a non-western tribal community adopts a new well-drilling technology. This new technology, a change in their material culture, may in turn lead them to new ways of farming with irrigation. This in turn might have a profound effect on their notions of diet, food gathering, and family organization. Thus, a change in material culture affected the development of the nonmaterial culture. However, when the technology was first adopted, changes in the nonmaterial elements (such as diet, food gathering, and family organization) lagged behind changes in the material elements.

CHAPTER 4

Socialization and the Self

Human beings have not been gifted with a wide range of instincts. In order to meet even their basic needs, they have learned to depend on each other and to cooperate. What makes human cooperation and interdependence possible is a system of learned behavioral patterns that are shared by the members of a culture. From a very early age, the human child acquires culturally approved norms, and in doing so begins the process of socialization.

This chapter explores the formal and informal agents of socialization and the consequences of this lifetime process. It shows how, through socialization, individuals develop a sense of self, acquire status, and take on a series of roles.

Socialization

Socialization is the process through which a human being learns the way of life of his/her society and develops the capacity to function both as an individual and as a member of the group. Although socialization begins at birth with the care of the newborn infant, it is a life-long process, occurring at all ages and stages in life.

Goals of Socialization

The following are the basic goals of the socialization process:

1. The individual must be taught the necessary skills demanded for living in his/her society.

2. The individual must be able to communicate effectively and develop the ability to speak, read, and write.

3. The individual must internalize the basic values and beliefs of the society.

4. The individual must develop a sense of self. The individual learns to view himself/herself as a distinct entity, apart from all other people and things.

Agents of Socialization

Socialization may take place through both formal and informal means. Educational and religious institutions, as well as the military, are examples of the formal, more structured agencies responsible for transmitting the accepted ways of acting and thinking within a society. Informal methods of socialization include interaction with peers, family, and the media. The major informal and formal agents of socialization—the family, the school, peer groups, and the mass media—are discussed below.

Family

The process of socialization begins within the family. Infants are totally dependent on those around them for food, clothing, and shelter. Equally important, however, is their need for love, attention, and physical contact. This emotional and physical dependency creates a strong attachment to their caregivers. To young children, therefore, the family represents the whole world around them. Thus, their perception of themselves, the world, and the people with whom they come in contact is directly influenced by their families' attitudes and beliefs. Parents teach their children these attitudes and values and impart information about the world through both verbal and nonverbal communication. In sum, the values that an individual has and the various roles that person is expected to play are initially learned within the family setting.

The social class of the family may influence the socialization process. Various studies suggest that middle-class and lower-class families differ in the methods and goals of disciplining their children. Working-class parents tend to utilize physical punishment, whereas middle-class parents use psychological methods (guilt, embarrassment). Furthermore, working-class parents place a high value on obedience, discipline, cleanliness, respect, and conformity to traditional standards of behavior. Middle-class families, on the other hand, place more emphasis on the child's motives for behaving in a given manner rather than on the behavior itself. Middle-class children are encouraged to be innovative and independent rather than to follow others. The social class of the family, then, affects the method and content of the messages in the socialization process.

Schools

In less technologically advanced societies, the family is primarily responsible for the socialization of the young. In technologically advanced societies, however, this responsibility is shared with formal organizations such as the school. The school is the agency primarily responsible for transmitting the accumulated knowledge and ways of a society to its young people once they reach five or six years of age. As an agent of socialization, the school is highly structured and organized around a set of rules that everyone is expected to obey. The school is also structured so that each grade or course leads logically to the next. Formal education is so important that entry into many professions is determined by successful completion of a required course of study.

Peer Groups

Although the major function of the peer group may be recreational, next to the family it is probably the most influential agent of socialization. Since peers are relatively equal, they usually share a common standing as they relate to persons in authority. As an agent of socialization, the peer group is most influential during adolescence, when young people spend a large portion of the day in the company of their friends. Adolescents often create a small culture of their own with its own jargon and values different from those of adult culture. In adolescence, popularity becomes an important goal, and to internalize and express the values of the peer group greatly contributes to one's acceptance. Teenagers who use the accepted jargon, wear the "right" clothes, and live up to the values of the peer group receive the most approval from their friends.

Mass Media

The mass media play an important role in socialization in American society. Most Americans spend significant time reading or viewing books, newspapers, television, radio, magazines, and movies. From the age of three through sixteen, the average child spends more time in front of the television than in the classroom. Such extensive exposure has given this medium a most influential role in socialization. Not only can the mass media reinforce cultural norms (e.g., public service announcements, educational television programs), it can also distort norms by giving young people the impression that what is transmitted or printed is a true reflection of society (e.g., soap operas). The values in the media are often in direct opposition to the messages given to young people by other agents of socialization.

The Development of the Self

Through socialization the individual learns to view himself/herself as a distinct entity, apart from all other people and things. The self has a personal identity, and others respond to it. The infant has no concept of self at birth, and awareness of his/her own being develops as part of socialization.

The Looking-Glass Self

The sociologist Charles Horton Cooley[1] formulated the theory of the "looking-glass self." The looking glass symbolizes society, which acts as a mirror that makes it possible to observe the reactions of others

---

1   Charles Horton Cooley, *Human Nature and the Social Order* (New York: Scribner's, 1902).

to our own behavior. We then interpret these reactions and incorporate this information in our concepts of self. An individual's self-concept is not only shaped by interactions with others, it also plays an important part in determining how an individual is likely to act in social relationships. In sum, the self is both a result of social interaction and an influence on social interaction.

The development of the social self begins in infancy and continues throughout life as the person comes in contact with new people and groups. Individuals develop the ability to look at themselves objectively and to make certain evaluations of themselves. They begin to recognize themselves as both the actors and the objects of evaluation.

The Generalized Other

The concept of the "generalized other" was developed by George Herbert Mead.[2] The generalized other is a composite of the expectations an individual believes others hold toward him/her. The individual examines himself/herself as though he/she were another person. Through the process of role-taking, the individual's awareness of this generalized other is developed.

As children develop communication skills, they begin to engage in role-taking. For example, a child can pretend that she is a teacher who is giving a lesson in spelling to the students (herself included). As she assumes this new role, she temporarily takes on the characteristics of the teacher and begins to have a clearer understanding of the teacher's methods, orientation, and attitudes.

Significant Others

Persons who exercise major influence over the attitudes of individuals are called significant others. An effort is made to please the significant others and to follow their advice and direction. For example, the softball coach will in all likelihood serve as a significant other to his/her players. The coach will instruct the players and try to set an

2   George Herbert Mead, *Mind, Self and Society* (Chicago: University of Chicago, 1934).

example for them to follow. In turn, the players will follow the instructions given by the coach and try to please him/her.

When we are infants, our significant others are usually limited to our parents, but the number of people who are important to us becomes greater as we grow older.

Status

Status refers to the social position that an individual holds in a group or the social ranking of a group when compared with other groups. An individual's status dictates the rights and privileges to which that person is entitled.

Ascribed Status

Ascribed status is acquired by the individual at birth. Wealth, religion, race, ethnic background, and social standing are all acquired as a consequence of being born into a particular family. Ascribed status is attained because of who you are, rather than what you have done. For example, a child born into a royal family will acquire a specific ascribed status that is not achieved by his/her own efforts. At birth the child is given a title and will be in a position superior to most people with whom he/she will have contact. For a royal child, the years ahead are well planned, with little room for individual choice.

Achieved Status

Achieved status is the status acquired because of what you have done through your own efforts or choice. For example, the student who works hard and completes the necessary further education or experience to attain a desired position is on his/her way to achieving a specific status position. Hard work, however, is not always a prerequisite to an achieved status. We can also achieve status with little effort, and some of these statuses will be negatively valued by particular groups (e.g., criminal).

Status Inconsistency

Historically, in most societies, the statuses that an individual held were fairly consistent. A person's occupation, ethnic background, and social class all fit together. However, in modern industrial society, where a status is determined by both ascription and achievement, an individual may hold a number of different statuses at the same time. These simultaneous statuses may be incompatible with one another because of conflicting expectations. This condition is referred to as status inconsistency. Individuals who experience status inconsistency may react by identifying with each conflicting status, by denying their association with the lower status group, or by becoming confused and uneasy.

Role

Role refers to the behaviors expected by others of one who holds a certain status or position. The appropriate roles are learned as part of the socialization process and then internalized by the individual. For example, within the faculty of a given university, a status system exists based in part on the rank and seniority of each professor. Typically, the senior full professor will be at the highest point, and the first-year instructor will occupy the lowest position. The senior full professor is expected to assume a leadership role among the faculty, have an outstanding publishing record, and secure more grant money for the university. The instructor, on the other hand, must prove himself/herself worthy of continuance, must show deference to the senior faculty, and must attempt to develop a "reputation" among colleagues in the field.

Reference Groups

Reference groups serve three important functions.

1. They set standards for how individuals should behave in different roles.

2. They serve a comparative function; an individual evaluates his/her individual role performance by making comparisons with others who are performing a similar task.

3. They serve as an audience for evaluating and making judgments about how individuals are performing in their roles.

As the person's own role in society changes, so will the reference groups against which she/he is measured.

Role Characteristics

There is a comprehensive terminology that sociologists use when examining roles and role behaviors. This section describes characteristics of roles and how they influence individual behavior.

Prescribed and Enacted Roles

The manner in which society expects us to carry out a particular role is referred to as the prescribed role. Even though some people do not always behave in a manner consistent with the expectations of others, we still see them as acting in a socially defined role. An enacted role is the way in which a person actually carries out a particular role. The discrepancy between the prescribed role and the enacted role may be due to one or more of the following: (1) a lack of understanding on the part of the individual as to what the role requires, (2) a wish not to conform to the expected requirements of the role, or (3) an inability on the part of the individual to play the role effectively.

Role Identity

Individuals occupy several different roles depending on the number of their social positions. We construct identities of ourselves while enacting these social roles. A role identity is the self concept we have as we are enacting a specific role. When individuals are asked to describe "who they are," they respond with identities connected to specific major roles in their lives (e.g., daughter, mother, student, etc.).

Role Distance

An individual who performs a particular role in an emotionally detached manner is displaying role distance. This often occurs when the role is not a high priority in the individual's life. Performance of the role is often accompanied by psychological strain, which may continue until the individual changes his/her priorities or redefines the role as something positive.

Role Strain

An individual having difficulty in a role because of ambiguous obligations or expectations pertaining to that role may experience role strain. For example, the manager of a department store who is expected to have good rapport with his/her employees and trainees is also expected to enforce the policy decisions of upper management and even to recommend firing an employee if she/he is not meeting expectations. To be "one of the gang" and at the same time enforce discipline may lead to role strain for a manager.

Role Conflict

An individual occupying one or more roles with contradictory or conflicting behavioral expectations is likely to experience role conflict. Modern industrial society is characterized by multiple group memberships, and most individuals are expected to fulfill the requirements of more than one role. For example, suppose a woman is the mother of two children, attends school, and also has a part-time job. This woman has several roles to play (mother, student, and worker). Her employers may expect her to work every day, even if she has a sick child at home or has exams coming up. At these times, she experiences role conflict, because of the contradictory or conflicting behavioral role expectations.

It is also possible for a person to experience conflict within a single role; behavioral expectations in a role may not agree with each other. For example, college professors are expected to devote a good deal of time and energy to their students—preparing lectures and meeting with them after class. In order to qualify for promotion and tenure, however, they are also expected to do research, publish, serve on faculty committees, and freely give a portion of their time to community organizations. These role behaviors (all within a single role) can often conflict.

Dramatic Role Presentation

An individual who makes a conscious attempt to play a role to its fullest in order to impress others is playing out a dramatic role presentation. This person often views the people with whom he/she interacts as if they were an audience, watching him/her perform. If the individual makes a conscious effort to put forth a desired image of himself/herself, and this image is accepted by the audience, then the objective of the role presentation is attained.

In the course of our normal activities, we all at some time play our role so as to impress those who are watching. The halfback running into the end zone for a touchdown and then slamming the ball to the ground, the attorney cross-examining a hostile witness, and the professor giving a flamboyant lecture in class are all examples of people in dramatic role presentations.

Learning New Roles Throughout a Lifetime

From infancy through old age, socialization continues. As individuals grow older and experience both positive and negative transitions (such as marriage, grandparenthood, impending death), new and changing roles, norms, and expectations emerge. The following list highlights some of the periods during which socialization or resocialization takes place.

1. Infancy to childhood

2. Childhood to adolescence

3. Adolescence to late teens to adulthood

4. Completion of formal education

5. Marriage

6. Parenthood

7. Separation

8. Divorce

9. Occupational change

10. Death of a parent

11. Retirement

12. Death of a spouse

CHAPTER 5

Sexuality and Gender Roles

Society not only shapes our sexual attitudes and behavior, it defines the roles that we as males and females in society are expected to play. Gender roles are the societal expectations attached to being male or female. Through gender-role socialization, children learn at an early age the behaviors expected of them.

This chapter presents four different approaches to the study of human sexual behavior: sociobiological, psychoanalytic, learning, and sociological. It then discusses changing attitudes and standards of sexual behavior and the ways in which children learn about sexuality and assume gender roles. The chapter concludes with a discussion of sexual orientation.

Theoretical Perspectives on Sexuality

Sexuality is defined as the sexual feelings and drives as well as the sexual practices common to a society. It is part of the broad spectrum of human behavior studied by sociologists. There is some debate as to whether sexual behavior is innate or learned. Are the behaviors and attitudes linked to sex basically biological processes, or are they socially learned from the environment? There are four main approaches to this question: sociobiological, psychoanalytic, learning, and sociological.

Sociobiological Approach

Sociobiology is the study of the biological basis of social behavior. Sociobiologists examine sexual behavior, one form of social behavior, by tracing the evolution of certain sexual patterns in humans as a species, not as individuals. They assert that certain sexual behaviors emerge and are maintained because they have been selected through evolutionary means as being most advantageous for members of the species to reproduce and pass on their genes. Consequently, sexual behavior is genetically programmed, and passing on one's genes is its main goal. The sociobiological perspective has been much criticized, however, because it fails to take into account the importance of culture, society, and learning in human sexuality.

Psychoanalytic Approach

Sigmund Freud, the father of psychoanalytic theory, asserted that two instincts motivate human behavior, the life instinct (which includes the sex drive, labeled *libido*) and the death instinct (labeled *thanatos*). Freud believed that society and individuals can and do sublimate or redirect the sex drive, the libidinal energy. The direction taken by this energy is influenced by three components of the human personality: the id, the ego, and the superego.

Components of the Personality

The *id*, present at birth, acts on the pleasure principle. It attempts to release instinctual tension and gratify the instinctual drives. The *ego*, on the other hand, is influenced by the constraints of the external world and develops later as the individual interacts with the rational world around him/her. The ego, acting on the reality principle, attempts to keep the pleasure-oriented id in line. The *superego* develops as the individual learns societal values and norms. It is the individual's moral conscience. Acting on the perfection principle, the superego strives to evaluate whether a specific act or attitude is morally right or wrong.

Psychosexual Stages

Freud held that sexual experiences in childhood shape adult sexual behavior and personality. Furthermore, there is a universal development of sexuality; all children pass through five psychosexual stages: oral stage, anal stage, phallic stage, latency stage, and genital stage. During each stage, the child's libidinal attention is focused on a different erogenous zone.

Criticisms of Freud's Theory

Freud's theory of sexuality is criticized for its overemphasis of the biological determinants of behavior, and not taking into account the roles of environment and learning. Another limitation stems from the fact that Freud developed his theory, in most part, as a result of therapy with disturbed patients. Because many of the theory's crucial constructs are unconscious components of the personality, they are hard to test empirically for their validity. Freud is also criticized for his implicit assumption that women are biologically inferior. In psychoanalytic theory, when girls realize that they lack a penis they go through a stage of "penis envy," and fail to develop as strong a superego as boys. Freud also believed that vaginal orgasm is more mature than clitoral orgasm. To feminists, Freud's theory is inadequate because it is basically male-centered.

Learning Approaches

While the previous two approaches assume that much of sexuality is innate, learning-oriented theorists hold that sexual behavior is largely influenced by learning processes. Early learning theorists discussed the acquisition of sexuality in terms of conditioning, both classical and operant. Social learning theorists extend the conditioning approaches and emphasize identification and the imitation of the sexual behavior of others.

Classical Conditioning

Classical conditioning explains why certain stimuli come to be sexually arousing. In classical conditioning, when a neutral stimulus is repeatedly paired with a stimulus that is sexually arousing, the previously neutral stimulus can elicit sexual arousal. For example, a person who has had some pleasant sexual experiences with a partner while lying on a fur rug may feel aroused by the sight of the rug alone. The principles of classical conditioning are often used to explain sexual fetishes, in which an individual becomes sexually aroused to variant stimuli other than another person.

Operant Conditioning

In operant conditioning, sexual behavior is learned and modified by the consequences of behavior. Behavior that is rewarded is likely to be repeated, whereas behavior that is punished (or not rewarded) is less likely to reoccur. For example, if a woman is rewarded for taking birth control pills by receiving approval and praise from her partner, feeling healthy when taking the pills, and reducing her chances of becoming pregnant, she is more likely to use the pills. On the other hand, if a woman experiences nausea and discomfort every time she takes a birth control pill, she will probably not take the pills consistently or will decide not to use them at all. However, research suggests that punishment after a specific behavior is not as effective as positive reinforcement in eliminating sexual behaviors. For example, children are often punished for masturbating in public. Nevertheless, most continue to masturbate, but they learn to do it where they are not likely to be caught.

Social Learning Approach

Both classical and operant conditioning consider the individual as a reactor to society, neglecting the fact that he/she is also an actor. Bandura's theory of social learning relies on the principles of early learning theory, recognizing their importance, but it doesn't ignore the important role that interaction plays in the learning of sexual behaviors. Besides conditioning, social learning theory postulates the existence of two other principles during the learning of sexual behaviors: identification and imitation. Individuals may identify with those around them (particularly important in the development of gender identity) and watch to see what sexual behaviors are rewarded. They learn new behaviors by imitating the behaviors of those around them.

Sociological Approaches

The theoretical approaches to the study of sexual behavior

described in this section are sociological. Note, however, that sociologists borrow principles and mechanisms from many of the other previously mentioned theoretical approaches. Just because an approach is psychological in nature, and developed by a psychologist, does not mean that sociologists do not agree with some of its facets.

Symbolic Interactionism

This sociological approach to sexual behavior, originated by George Herbert Mead,[1] states that the meaning of objects (including sex) is not inherent in the objects themselves; rather, it is created and taught in the context of social interaction. According to symbolic interactionism, sexual behavior is not just an expression of biological instincts, merely a response to stimuli, nor simply imitations of the behavior of others, but a product of interaction and communication between people. We attach sexual meaning to behavior and to ourselves by observing others and their reactions and labels to our behaviors.

Interacting with others, we take on roles or socially defined positions. In playing these roles, we learn a series of "scripts" or behavioral expectations about how to interact in these roles. These scripts help us to define certain situations as sexual or not. For example, a specific script exists for a woman at a gynecological exam. During the exam, the doctor examines the woman's breasts and genitalia, but the woman does not interpret this as sexual. The roles of doctor and patient do not give sexual meaning to this situation. A script supplies information that helps define the situation (Is this a seductive situation?), appropriate actors in the situation (Is my doctor an appropriate person?), and appropriate guidelines for interaction (Does this situation allow for sexual activity?).

Symbolic interactionism has been criticized for not truly explaining spontaneous sexual behavior and sexual behavior that occurs in ambiguous situations. If an individual has no script to give meaning to a situation, then how does he/she come to define it as sexual? Furthermore, it may be difficult (although not impossible) for individuals to interact with others who have different scripts for the same situation.

---

1   George Herbert Mead, *Mind, Self and Society* (Chicago: University of Chicago, 1934).

Differences in sexual scripts is often given as the reason why date rape occurs. One person defines the situation as sexual, while the other member does not.

Functionalism

This sociological approach to the study of sexual behavior views society as made up of several parts with specific functions. According to functionalism, society is in a state of equilibrium and is organized to maintain this order and stability. Sexuality can disrupt this order; therefore, social institutions must regulate sexual behavior through laws, beliefs, norms, and so on. Functionalists study the process by which sexuality is controlled and how this regulation affects the sexual behavior and attitudes of individuals.

Sexual Attitudes and Behaviors

Attitudes toward sexuality are shaped by several different sources in society. At an early age, parents and religion play important roles in the sexual socialization of children, establishing conservative standards of behavior. As children enter adolescence, their peers and dating partners become more influential and have a permissive effect. When young people become parents themselves, they tend to become sexually conservative again. Not unexpectedly, research suggests that young adults who have a close relationship with their parents retain more conservative standards throughout their lifetime.

Standards of sexual behavior, however, change with the times. In the past several decades, for example, there has been a shift in the attitude toward premarital intercourse. Ira Reiss,[2] a sociologist, established four categories of standards regarding premarital sex:

1. *Abstinence.* Premarital intercourse is not allowable. This standard holds true for males as well as females. Sex is allowable only in the context of marriage.

2. *Permissiveness with Affection.* Premarital intercourse is permis-

---

2   Ira L. Reiss, *Premarital Sexual Standards in American* (New York: Free Press, 1960).

sible if there is a strong emotional tie between the two people. The context must be a strong and stable relationship.

3. *Permissiveness without Affection.* Premarital intercourse is permissible if both people want it. The context need not be an emotional and stable relationship.

4. *Double Standard.* Premarital intercourse is okay for males, but not for females. The "orthodox" double standard states that this holds true regardless of the type of relationship. The "transitional" double standard states that premarital intercourse is okay if the woman is in an emotional and stable relationship.

The recent shift in the standards of premarital sexuality, especially among young people, is from abstinence to permissiveness with affection. Some evidence suggests that the double standard still exists, yet where it persists it has shifted from the orthodox double standard to a transitional double standard.

Statistics on sexual behavior bear out this shift in attitude. There is currently a higher incidence of premarital intercourse, especially among women, than in the 1940s, as recorded in the Kinsey Report. Furthermore, the age at which first intercourse occurs is decreasing.

Attitudes toward premarital sexuality have changed in Western society for several reasons: (1) religion, which has a conservative effect on sexual standards, has declined in Western society, (2) parents have become more permissive in their sexual standards, and (3) young people have become more independent and more age segregated and thus more subject to the permissive influence of peers. However, the spread of sexually transmitted diseases, including AIDS, may be changing this permissive trend.

Sexuality Education

Individuals acquire information on sexuality from both informal and formal sources in society.

Informal Sexuality Education

Parents teach their children, both directly and indirectly, about sexual behavior as well as attitudes and values regarding sexuality. Young people acquire most of their sexual information from peers, although some of this information is inaccurate. The mass media, especially television, advertisements, films, and popular music, are another informal source of sexual information for young people.

Formal Sexuality Education

Sexuality teaching in the schools has been widely debated. Although most parents approve of some form of sexuality education in the classroom, the content and goals of these classes are controversial. The main concern is the effect that sexuality education may have on the attitudes and behavior of the students. Will young people who learn about sexuality and contraception in a classroom become sexually active or more sexually active because of this information?

First, research suggests that students do not change their personal standards as a result of a sexuality education program. They do, however, become more tolerant of variant sexual behaviors in others. Second, students do not become more experimental and promiscuous. Sexuality education does appear to increase both masturbatory and orgasm experiences, but researchers suggest that such courses relieve anxiety and fears concerning these topics, thereby facilitating communication between partners and/or allowing people to participate in these behaviors. Finally, sexuality education programs that include on-site contraceptive clinics influence the contraceptive behaviors of students. Students who participate in these clinic-oriented programs use birth control more often and use more effective contraceptive methods.

Gender Roles

Gender roles are the socially constructed behavioral expectations for males and females. These role-specific expectations are traditionally quite different for males and females. For example, males have been expected to be strong, unemotional, career oriented, and aggressive; females, weak, emotional, relationship/family oriented, and dependent. When individuals behave according to gender-role expectations, it is usually because of traditional gender-role socialization.

Gender-Role Socialization

Gender-role socialization is the process by which males and females learn the behaviors that are expected of them in society. This socialization begins in childhood, when children are rewarded for their gender-oriented behavior (what a pretty dress you have on) and punished or embarrassed for non-gender-oriented behavior (little boys don't play with dolls). This gender-role socialization is a life-long process, however, and does not stop once an individual becomes an adult (women should stay home when their children are young, men should go out and make the money).

Research regarding gender stereotypes suggests that individuals, both young and old, still typify males and females according to gender-role trait expectations. There is some evidence, however, that gender-role attitudes changed in the 1970s (toward more egalitarian, liberal attitudes) but leveled off in the 1980s.

Past research examining gender roles assumed that individuals were either "masculine" (adhered to the male gender role) or "feminine" (adhered to the female gender role). Furthermore, if an individual adhered to one of these orientations, he/she could not adhere to the other. Current research by Sandra L. Bem[3] and others reports that many people are psychologically androgynous, that is, they possess both masculine and feminine gender-role characteristics at the same time. This current research sheds light on the fact that males and females do not fall on a unidimensional trait continuum whereby one extreme is feminine (with the exclusion of masculine traits) and the other extreme is masculine (with the exclusion of feminine traits). Males and females turn out to be non-unidimensional with the possibility of being very masculine, very feminine, both feminine and masculine (androgynous), or possessing neither masculine nor feminine traits.

Gender Differences/Similarities

Do psychological differences exist between the genders? Males and females do seem to differ in areas such as aggressiveness, self-esteem,

3   Sandra L. Bem, "The Measurement of Psychological Androgyny," *Journal of Consulting and Clinical Psychology*, 42:155-162 (1974).

and ease or willingness to self-disclose. It is difficult, however, to determine whether these differences are inherent, biological differences or are the result of social learning, environment, socialization, and structural processes. Furthermore, researchers suggest that although there may be differences in communication styles and personality, gender similarity is more common than gender difference.

Sexual Orientation

Sexual identity refers to the identity (or concept of self) one has, based on one's sexual orientation. Sexual orientation refers to a behavioral orientation; whether one is heterosexual (sexual relations with the opposite gender), homosexual (sexual relations with same gender), or bisexual (sexual relations with the same and the opposite gender). One should not confuse the term "gender identity" (one's concept of self as being masculine or feminine) with "sexual identity" (one's concept of self as homosexual, heterosexual, or bisexual). Lesbians and gays differ from heterosexuals in their choice of sexual partners but they do not necessarily differ in their gender-role identities.

Several theories attempt to explain why individuals are heterosexual, homosexual, or bisexual in orientation. Biological theories involve hormonal imbalance or a genetic predisposition. Psychoanalytic theories suggest that gay and lesbian sexuality is an inappropriate fixation at one psychosexual stage, or a continuation of the love for one's same-sex parent. Learning theorists postulate that early childhood sexual experiences shape future adult sexual behavior; children are born with no predisposition toward heterosexuality, bisexuality, or homosexuality. Sociological theorists point to the importance of labeling in the process of forming one's sexual orientation; if one is labeled as heterosexual or homosexual, one begins to act in accordance with that label.

In actuality, however, we don't know why people are the way they are. No single factor in any of these theories is the cause of sexual orientation. This suggests that the determinants of sexual orientation are different for different individuals.

CHAPTER 6

Deviance and Social Control

As defined in Chapter 4, socialization is the process through which individuals learn the values and norms of the society in which they live and develop the capacity to function both as individuals and as members of society. Oftentimes, however, individuals fail to conform to the norms and expectations of a group or of society at large. To maintain the necessary level of social organization in a society, mechanisms are developed to control any deviant behavior that occurs or threatens to occur.

This chapter provides some reasons why individuals deviate from the norms of society and explains how society deals with these norm violations. It considers first the internalization of societal norms and the kinds of external social control mechanisms that come into play when the internalization process fails. It then takes a close look at deviant behavior—its relationship to social control mechanisms, the theories that attempt to explain it, and its implications for both society and the individual.

Social Control

Through socialization, a person learns what behavior is acceptable in various situations and learns to differentiate between proper and improper behavioral patterns. Social controls extend this process. Society cannot function smoothly unless its members conform to the norms, carry out their roles, and coordinate their activities so that group or societal goals can be achieved.

Social Norms and Social Control

The aim of social control is to ensure that the members of a society conform to existing social norms. Social norms define what kinds of behaviors individuals are expected to display or to avoid in particular social situations. There are no absolute norms by which one can judge another person's conduct. People in different societies abide by different norms, as do various groups within a single society. Norms change in all societies over time, so behaviors must be judged in relation to the time and place in which they occur. For example, codes of dress have changed, and laws that once forbade the consumption of alcohol and the use of certain drugs have now been repealed or modified.

Forms of Social Norms

Social norms may take one of the following four forms:

1. *Values:* deep-seated sentiments shared by members of a society

2. *Folkways:* customary, habitual ways of acting

3. *Mores:* the more important folkways, carrying significant implications of right and wrong

4. *Laws:* mores of particular significance that have been formalized and hold out the threat of legal punishment for their violation

Proscribed and Prescribed Norms

Norms may also be either proscribed or prescribed. A proscribed norm specifies something that an individual must not do, such as taking another person's life, engaging in incest, and driving on the wrong side of the road. A prescribed norm, on the other hand, specifies those things that an individual should do, such as taking care of one's children, paying bills on time, and wearing proper attire.

Conflicting Social Norms

Because of multiple group membership, which is characteristic of life in an industrial society, each of us is expected to conform to a rather large number of norms, some of which may be in conflict with one another. When norms do come into conflict, those that hold the greatest importance to the individual will be observed, while the others will at least temporarily be set aside. Thus, there will be times when one must analyze a particular situation to determine what behavior is in order. When situations of this type emerge, our internal mechanisms for social control may temporarily be thrown into a state of confusion. For example, a business executive who happens to be extremely religious may experience a conflict of norms. His/her religion teaches the virtues of charity, sympathy, honesty, and sincerity, yet the realities of the business world may dictate behavior that is in conflict with these religious norms. When a particular situation brings these two sets of values into conflict, the executive must decide which ones to abide by and which to leave behind.

Similarly, friends and family may expect us to behave in contradictory ways. The friends of a teenage boy, for example, may think it proper and adultlike for him to stay out late, smoke, and drink alcoholic beverages, while his parents may consider these activities wrong for someone his age.

Internal Social Controls

Social control is really an extension of the socialization process. To maintain the necessary level of social organization and order in a society, behavior that has become patterned and predictable must be continued. To accomplish this end, all societies socialize their members so that they will behave in a socially acceptable manner. If socialization is effectively exerted, the individual internalizes the norms of a culture and does not have to stop and think about what is right or wrong, proper or improper—he/she follows the norms almost as a matter of reflex. When people have internalized norms, they do not conform because they fear punishment. Rather, they conform because they would feel guilty or ashamed if they engaged in improper behavior even if they were not observed or caught. Most necessary social controls are exercised internally by each of us.

External Social Controls

When the socialization process fails and individuals do not internalize the norms of society, external social control mechanisms are used to maintain the necessary order. Some individuals do not feel guilt, shame, or remorse when breaking important rules or regulations. A paid killer, for example, is someone who has been improperly or incompletely socialized: he/she usually expresses no feelings of regret or shame after committing the crime. For such individuals, conformity to social norms must be secured through external controls such as ridicule, ostracism, and physical punishment. When external pressures are used, people are compelled to conform out of fear of possible punishment or ridicule. External social control can be exerted by both informal and formal mechanisms.

Informal Social Control

Informal social control is very apparent within the primary group, which may be the family, a friendship group, a work group, or some other social group. In most instances, we assume responsibility for exerting some control over another individual because of the particular role we occupy in relation to that individual. A large range of informal mechanisms for maintaining social control are available. These include ostracism, gossip, ridicule, laughter, or the threat of any of these. The fear of group disapproval is an effective social control mechanism because acceptance is so vital. The mere chance of losing the acceptance of the group may be enough to make the person conform.

Formal Social Control

Formalized social control may be exerted by a large number of social institutions, organizations, and agencies within a society. These organizations include, but are not limited to, schools, police agencies, prisons, juvenile detention centers, courts, institutions for the mentally ill, and social welfare agencies. The major system of formal social control in American society is the criminal justice system.

Each formal control system has a set of formal control mechanisms, which are those written rules, regulations, codes of behavior, and laws that specify in writing how procedures should be carried out, how individuals occupying specific roles should behave, and what form of punishment or penalty will be imposed on those who disobey. Through the application of these formal mechanisms, for example, the criminal may be imprisoned, the psychotic hospitalized, and the drug abuser placed on probation. It is hoped that just the threat of imprisonment or probation will deter those who might want to deviate from the existing norms of society.

Sanctions

Every society has developed a system of rewards and punishments (both considered sanctions) in order to encourage its members to conform to existing norms. Positive sanctions are those rewards given when one conforms to existing norms. Negative sanctions are the punishments that may be applied when an individual fails to conform. Both informal and formal agents of social control use positive and negative sanctions. Many sociologists believe that the informal rewards and punishments are often more effective than the formal sanctions, and they are certainly applied more often.

When children enter school, they learn to abide by the rules and accept the dominant values. If the child conforms, he/she will be rewarded. The rewards may take the form of acceptance (by teachers and other students), good marks, popularity, and promotion to the next grade. If the child fails to conform, he/she may be rejected by teachers and students, earn poor marks, and be left back a grade at the end of the year. Thus, schools exert social control through both formal (grades, promotion) and informal (popularity, rejection) mechanisms.

Just as socialization is a life-long process, so too is social control. The agents of social control may vary, but the process of inducing individuals to conform, through both formal and informal methods, continues throughout a lifetime.

Deviant Behavior

To sociologists, the term "deviance" refers to any behavior that fails to conform to the expectations of society or a given group within society. Deviance is a departure from the norm by an individual or a group. Examples of deviance in our own culture include murder, child abuse, rape, robbery, insanity, mental illness, juvenile delinquency, white-collar crime, alcoholism, drug addiction, and prostitution.

Deviant behavior and deviant acts are defined by the social norms existing within a culture. An act that may be proper and acceptable in one situation may be improper and unacceptable in another. For instance, the police officer who shoots and kills an escaped murderer as a last resort (in an act of self-defense) may receive a citation of merit for his bravery. However, the criminal who shoots and kills a person during a holdup is subject to some of the most severe penalties that may be inflicted under the law. In both instances, the same behavior occurs, but in one situation the behavior is acceptable and in the other it is not.

The Individual Deviant

When a person who is acting alone deviates from the established norms of his/her subculture and in fact rejects those norms, we consider that person an individual deviant. The rapist who works alone, seeks out his victim, and finally commits the crime is an example of an individual deviant. He does not plan and execute the crime with anyone else but rather acts in a solitary manner.

Group Deviation

A group that acts as a collective entity in a manner contrary to the norms of the conventional society is displaying group deviation. A large amount of group deviation takes place within society's deviant subcultures. It should be emphasized that the individual in this situation behaves in conformity with the norms of the subculture; it is the subculture that has rejected the norms of the society. A delinquent gang exemplifies the concept of group deviation. The gang has its own set of norms, values, attitudes, and traditions. The gang member who adheres to the rules of the gang is conforming to the expectations of his/her peers, but the gang as a collectivity is not conforming to the standards of the conventional society.

Deviant Subcultures

A significant amount of deviant behavior takes place within the society's subcultures. Many individuals who have been rejected by conventional society seek the companionship of a deviant subculture in an attempt to find status, comfort, and acceptance. Once within the deviant subculture, they begin a socialization process in order to learn the accepted codes of behavior and assume their proper role. Deviant subcultures aid their members by protecting them from the larger society, giving them esteem and approval, teaching them how to engage in deviant acts and not be detected, and helping them to solve whatever problems they meet in trying to adapt to a style of life that is different from that found in conventional society.

Sociological Relevance

Sociologists study deviance to become familiar with the social and cultural forces that influence deviant acts. They also study the impact of deviance on a society and the effect on the individual of being labeled a deviant. They study the lifestyle of deviant individuals and deviant groups. In addition, they study those who are labeled deviant and why the label is given. Finally, sociologists study how widespread certain forms of deviance are and how society may alleviate the deviance or deal with it.

Explanations of Deviance

A number of theories have been devised to explain deviant behavior. The theories can be classified according to whether the variable explaining deviance is biological, psychological, or sociological in nature.

Biological Explanations

Biological theories attribute deviance to organic or physiological weaknesses. Scientists who subscribe to this school of thought believe that social deviance is positively related to biological factors such as body type and chromosome pattern. Biological explanations of deviance have been much criticized and have not attracted wide support.

Body-Type Theories.

Cesare Lombroso,[1] a nineteenth-century Italian criminologist, was the pioneer among those scientists who attempted to explain deviant behavior in terms of body type. In his writings, Lombroso suggested that the criminal is biologically less advanced than the normal citizen and would physically resemble his/her evolutionary ancestors more than his/her contemporaries. A person with excessively large jaws and cheekbones, eye defects or peculiarities, extremely long arms, large fingers and toes, and abnormal dentition would fit Lombroso's model of a criminal type. Charles Goring, a student of Lombroso's who continued this work after Lombroso died, found that there were no significant physical differences between criminals and the rest of the population.

William Sheldon,[2] an American physical anthropologist, identified three basic body types: the endomorph (round, soft, fat), the mesomorph (muscular, athletic), and the ectomorph (skinny, fragile, bony). Sheldon tried to correlate personality and behavior with body type. He concluded, as a result of his research, that the mesomorph was the type most likely to be delinquent, for mesomorphs were impulsive, energetic, and nervous. He found endomorphs to be friendly and self-indulgent, while ectomorphs were overly sensitive and somewhat withdrawn.

Using the typology developed by William Sheldon, Eleanor and Sheldon Glueck[3] in 1956 published the results of research in which they compared five hundred delinquent boys to five hundred nondelinquent boys. The Gluecks found that a statistically significant percentage of the delinquent boys were mesomorphs.

Although there is some empirical evidence for body-type theories,

1   Cesare Lombroso, in G.L Ferrero, *Criminal Man* (New York: Putnam, 1911) and Cesare Lombroso, *Crime: Its Causes and Remedies* (Boston: Little, Brown, 1918).
2   William H. Sheldon, *Varieties of Delinquent Youth* (New York: Harper and Brothers, 1949).
3   Sheldon and Eleanor Glueck, *Physique and Delinquency* (New York: Harper and Row, 1956).

studies used to support them have been criticized. These studies often fail to obtain representative samples (both control samples and subject samples), and the criteria for classification into one of the three body-type categories are often biased by the experimenter.

Chromosome Theories

Research on the relationship of certain sex chromosome patterns with deviant behavior is still being carried out, although there have been several convincing efforts to disprove any theory linking the two. A normal man has an XY chromosome pattern, a normal woman an XX pattern. Occasionally, males are born with an extra Y chromosome, giving them an XYY chromosome pattern that some researchers believe predisposes them to violent behavior. Richard Speck, a man convicted of killing seven nurses in Chicago in 1966, had an XYY chromosome pattern. This discovery spurred a good deal of research in the United States that attempted to find a correlation between this chromosome pattern and deviant behavior. Present research, however, has failed to confirm the double-Y chromosome hypothesis.

Psychological Explanations

Psychological theorists attribute deviance to personality problems or problems of individual adjustment. Certain types of personalities, they propose, tend to be more closely related to social deviance than are others.

Psychoanalytic Theories

As discussed earlier, Sigmund Freud divided the personality into three parts: the id, the ego, and the superego. The id represents the unconscious, instinctual, impulsive, and unsocialized part of the personality. The ego represents the conscious, rational part of the personality. The ego monitors the interaction between the id and the superego. The superego represents that part of the personality that has absorbed cultural values and functions as the conscience. Those subscribing to the psychoanalytic school believe that deviant behavior results when there is an overactive (and uncontrollable) id present in combination with an underactive superego, while at the same time the ego stands by and fails to give adequate direction.

Sociological Explanations

Sociologists have taken several different approaches to explain deviant behavior. One approach is to investigate the causes and incidence of deviant behavior. These theories focus on the norms and values of society and why rule violation occurs. Theories in this grouping include differential association, anomie, and control theory. Another approach focuses on how behaviors and persons get labeled deviant. Theories in this grouping include labeling theory and conflict theory.

Differential Association Theory

This theory, developed by the sociologist Edwin H. Sutherland,[4] assumes that for a person to be criminal, he/she must first learn how to be deviant. Definitions and beliefs about behavior vary from group to group and are learned through social interaction with other people. Most individuals are exposed to both deviant and nondeviant individuals or groups. Sutherland measured interaction with these groups in terms of the frequency, priority, duration, and intensity of contact with each group. The higher the level of each of these four variables to either the deviant or the nondeviant group, the greater the likelihood that the individual will learn the definitions of that group and will behave in a similar manner. Sutherland states that individuals engage in deviant behavior when the definitions favorable toward norm violation outweigh those unfavorable.

White-collar crime is a deviant practice that involves individuals of high social status and respectability who commit a crime in the normal course of their occupation. Examples include misrepresentation in advertising, fee-splitting, and price-fixing. Differential association theory states that in order to commit this type of crime, one has first to learn the proper motives and techniques of such behavior. By having frequent, long, and intense contact with colleagues who engage in this behavior, and by giving priority to the relationships established with these colleagues, individuals learn definitions favorable to these norm

---

4   Edwin H. Sutherland, *Principles of Criminology* (Philadelphia: Lippincott, 1939).

violations, and they soon begin to commit these criminal acts themselves.

There is much research support for differential association theory. Furthermore, some behavioral theorists have taken the theory one step further, by suggesting that reinforcement plays an important part in the learning of definitions. Individuals are likely to engage in deviant behavior if they learn definitions favorable to rule violation, and they are likely to continue engaging in this behavior if it is rewarding to them.

Anomie Theory

This theory explains deviance as the result of an existing strain between the culture and social structure of a society. Emile Durkheim introduced sociologists to the concept of anomie, which is defined as a state of normlessness or rootlessness that results when cultural expectations are inconsistent with social realities. Robert K. Merton[5] attempted to correlate anomie with social deviance. He assumed that as a result of socialization, individuals learn the significant cultural goals, while at the same time learning the culturally accepted means of achieving those goals. When opportunities to reach these goals are not present, and individuals seek alternatives, then the alternative behaviors may result in social deviancy.

Merton listed four types of deviant behavior that may emerge if anomie is present—innovation, ritualism, retreatism, and rebellion.

1. *Innovation.* Innovation occurs when people accept the cultural goals of a society but reject the culturally accepted means of achieving the goals. Bank robbers attempt to achieve the same goal as other members of society, the accumulation of wealth. However, rather than achieving wealth through conventional means (job, savings), bank robbers break the rules and try to obtain the goal illegitimately.

2. *Ritualism.* Ritualism takes place when a person accepts the culturally approved means but rejects the goals. A hospital attendant is a ritualist if he/she is more concerned with filling out a routine form

---

5   Robert K. Merton, *Social Theory and Social Structure* (Glencoe, IL.: Free Press, 1957).

for a patient in the emergency room than with providing swift medical treatment for that person.

3. *Retreatism*. Retreatism results when a person rejects both the culturally approved goals and the means of attaining those goals. An alcoholic who gives up family, job, friends, and hobbies to continue a life of drinking in solitude effectively retreats from conventional society.

4. *Rebellion*. Rebellion occurs when the culturally approved goals and means are rejected, and the individual tries to overthrow the existing system and replace it with new goals and means. The Black Panthers and the Weathermen, extremist groups that peaked in the 1960s, are examples of rebellious groups.

The type of behavior engaged in by an individual is a result of the illegitimate and legitimate opportunities available. These opportunities are often based on an individual's social status in society, either because of race, education, income, ethnicity, gender, or age. In order to engage in a particular behavior or role, whether legitimate or illegitimate, one must have the opportunity to engage in the role, and one must have learned how to behave in that role. The individual must have access to a *learning structure* where he/she can learn skills appropriate to a role, and an *opportunity structure* where he/she has the opportunity to participate in the role.

According to anomie theory, access to legitimate learning and opportunity structures is limited. Not all individuals, for example, have the skills or the opportunity to work at a conventional job. Furthermore, access to illegitimate learning and opportunity structures is also limited. Not all individuals have the skills necessary and the opportunity to be a successful thief or hired killer. In sum, deviant behavior, according to Merton, is a phenomenon that results from the lack of fit between the social structure and culture. The origin of deviance lies within the social organization of society rather than within the makeup of the individual.

Control Theory

Control theory states that social controls influence our behavior. Travis Hirschi[6] states that there is a bond between the individual and conventional society. The stronger the social bond, the greater the norms of society that have been internalized, and the less likely that an individual will deviate from those norms. Hirschi discusses the social bond in terms of four components.

1. *Attachment.* Attachment is one's affection and responsiveness to others, as well as one's sensitivity to their opinions. The greater the attachment, the more likely one is to internalize the norms of society.

2. *Belief.* Belief refers to the values themselves, which have been internalized. They usually consist of respect for others in authority. Deviance is less likely to occur if belief is strong.

3. *Commitment to the Long-Term Culturally Approved Goals of Society.* This is another aspect of the social bond. The greater the commitment to long-term educational and occupational goals, the less likely one is to deviate from those goals.

4. *Involvement.* Individuals who are involved in culturally approved activities in local institutions and organizations are less likely to deviate. For example, if a high school student is part of the choir, on the school volleyball team, and a member of the debate team, he/she is less likely to deviate from consensually held norms of behavior.

Comparison of Anomie, Control, and Differential Association Theories

Although anomie theory, control theory, and differential association theory differ in what variable is most important in determining deviant behavior, the perspectives are not incompatible. Anomie theory states that a discrepancy between culturally approved goals and legitimate means for achieving those goals is the factor that leads to deviance. Individuals learn the definitions of these goals and the appropriate means of achieving them either through their attachment to

6   Travis Hirschi, *Causes of Delinquency* (Berkeley: University of California Press, 1969).

conventional society (control theory), through interactions with deviant and nondeviant groups (differential association theory), or through the availability of learning and opportunity structures (anomie theory).

Labeling Theory

In contrast to anomie, control, and differential association theories, which are concerned with why rule violation occurs, labeling theory and its extension, conflict theory, examine how behaviors and persons get labeled deviant. Labeling theory assumes that deviance is relative. It is the reaction of others rather than the act itself that defines a behavior as deviant. A distinction is made between primary and secondary deviance.

Primary Deviance. Nearly every person has at one time or another behaved in a deviant manner. When an individual engages in deviant acts but the deviance is temporary and not recurrent, this is called primary deviance. The individual remains a socially acceptable person, one whose lifestyle is not dominated by a deviant pattern. Most often people ignore this type of deviance and do not label the person deviant. Furthermore, such a person will almost certainly not consider himself/herself a deviant. The person who occasionally cheats on his/her income tax, drives in excess of the speed limit, drinks too much at a party, or engages the services of a bookie is involved in the primary form of deviance.

Secondary Deviance. What happens to recurrent primary deviance depends on whether the behavior is caught and how others interpret the acts. If the individual characteristically shows deviant behavior, is publicly identified as a deviant, and organizes his/her life around the acts labeled deviant, then the individual is engaged in secondary deviance. Society finds such individuals unacceptable and undesirable. When the person who drinks too much at a party goes on to drink excessively at home, at work, and at other social events, and is recognized as an alcoholic, he/she enters the secondary stage of deviance.

According to labeling theory, once a deviant label is affixed to an individual, other people will deal with the person in terms of the label, and that label itself may have more significance than any other status the person holds. A person who views himself/herself in terms of the label may behave accordingly. After recognizing himself/herself as a deviant and being treated as such by others, this person may depart both socially and physically from conventional society and associate only with others who have been similarly labeled. At this point, the deviant label will have become a self-fulfilling prophecy; the reaction of others and the label itself will induce the exact behavior it is intended to label. For example, a youth who is caught shoplifting may be sent to prison or a juvenile detention center. After he gets out, he carries with him the label of deviant. The label itself, rather than subsequent deviant behavior, may prevent him from getting a job and may be the cause of his losing friends. Others may react to him only on the basis of this label. In time, the behaviors of others toward the label may cause him to behave in a manner that confirms the label.

Conflict Theory

Conflict theory is actually an extension of labeling theory, which holds that definitions of deviance are relative and it is the reactions of others rather than the behavior itself that define a behavior as deviant. Conflict theory takes this statement one step further and states that those individuals in power are the "others" who define what behaviors are deviant. Those with access to the means of production in a society have greater power, and therefore, they develop laws, social institutions, and deviant labels to protect their own interests and to continue the present social order. Consequently, white-collar crime—deviance usually engaged in by the higher socioeconomic classes—has a lower probability of being labeled deviant than does crime engaged in by those from the lower classes. Furthermore, drinking alcohol is not illegal because it is socially acceptable in the upper classes. Conflict theory, like anomie theory, suggests that the structure of society, rather than the individual, is responsible for deviance. As suggested by Marx, crime will continue as long as there is a conflict of interests in society.

Comparison of Labeling and Conflict Theories

Both labeling theory and conflict theory focus on the types of acts and the people who are labeled deviant. How acts come to be labeled and the consequences of this labeling process are the major concern of labeling theory, whereas the role of power and inequality in definitions of deviance is the focus of conflict theory. Both theories, however, have limitations. A major limitation to labeling theory is that it restricts itself to the reactions of others to deviance and does not attempt to explain the causes of primary deviance. Conflict theory fails to explain fully deviance that occurs within the classes of the powerful.

Official Statistics

Many deviant or criminal acts that occur are never reported to the authorities. Different areas in the United States have different definitions and requirements for deviant acts. Consequently, official statistics are a misleading indicator of the level of deviance present and the number of persons who are engaging in deviant acts. The Uniform Crime Reports, published by the Federal Bureau of Investigation, represent the most complete reporting of criminal statistics in the United States. However, these crime reports only include the number of offenses actually reported to the police. Crime in many categories is grossly underreported, including forcible rape, confidence games, and acts in which many believe that there is no victim (e.g., prostitution). (The phrase "victimless crime" is much debated among social scientists. Is there such a thing as a "victimless crime"? Even if both individuals participate freely, one person could still be labeled as a victim.) As methods of record keeping improve, however, it would appear that the level of deviancy would increase.

Part III:
Social Organization

Society is a complex system of individuals, groups of individuals, social institutions, and organizations. The previous section emphasized the individual, his/her relationship with society, and the process by which a person learns to become an acceptable member of society. This section focuses on the social organization of society in its many forms.

Chapter 7 is about groups in general—their nature, structure, and influence. Chapter 8 differentiates between social institutions and formal organizations. Marriage and the family as a social institution found in all societies is the subject of Chapter 9.

CHAPTER 7

Social Groups

Everyone is a member of groups, whether by choice or by circumstance, whether to serve personal or utilitarian needs. Groups may be large or small, formal or informal. This chapter is concerned with the nature of groups, the different kinds of groups that have sociological significance, how groups affect individual behavior, and the types of leaders that emerge in problem-solving groups.

Definition

Sociologists disagree about the criteria for labeling a group. Consequently, a student of sociology can discover several different meanings of "group" in textbooks and readings.

1. A group is any physical collection of people. The passengers together on an airplane, the spectators at a baseball game, and the shoppers standing in line at the checkout counter of a supermarket are all examples of this meaning of group. The only identifiable common denominator among these people is that they happen to be in the same place at the same time. Some sociologists, however,

would define this collection of people as a collectivity or aggregation of people, rather than as a group of people.

2.   A group is a number of people who share some common characteristic. People of the same age group, ethnic background, race, occupation, or sex would be members of the same group according to this definition. Other sociologists label this a category of people rather than a group of people.

3. A group is a number of people who share some organized pattern of recurrent interaction. Examples would be a church choir, high school club, union local, and PTA.

4. A group is any number of people interacting together who share a consciousness of membership based on shared expectations of behavior. This is perhaps the most acceptable definition. Here the criterion is neither physical proximity, similar characteristics, nor continuous interaction, it is a sense of common expectations. An example would be business associates from the same firm who get together at a meeting to decide which applicants should be hired for the next fiscal year. These business associates share common expectations about what will occur at the meeting.

Kinds of Groups

Sociologists have identified different types of groups, categorized according to specific characteristics: whether people choose to join a specific group, how individuals feel toward others inside and outside their groups, and the types of relationships that form within groups.

Voluntary and Involuntary Groups

An individual may choose the groups he/she wishes to join. These chosen groups are referred to as voluntary groups. Students at a university, adult members of a family, and registered Democrats are all members of voluntary groups. In other cases, however, individuals may be placed in groups through no choice of their own; these groups are referred to as involuntary groups. Soldiers drafted into the army and inmates at a prison are members of involuntary groups, since in most instances they did not elect to be there.

In-Groups and Out-Groups

Some groups are characterized by the sense of belongingness of its members. Groups to which an individual feels he/she belongs are called in-groups. Examples of in-groups are one's family, racial or ethnic group, and religious group. The groups to which an individual feels he/she does not belong are labeled as out-groups. Examples of out-groups are other families, other racial or ethnic groups, and other religious groups—groups of people with whom a person feels a lack of common interests.

Group Boundaries

Because members of in-groups usually feel comfortable in each other's presence and share common experiences, a feeling of "we-ness" develops. In order to maintain a distinction between the "we" of the group and the "they" who remain outside the group, boundaries are created. The boundaries that distinguish members from nonmembers may be either formal or informal. When formal boundaries are present, membership in the group is based on a predetermined criterion such as election into the group. Formal boundaries may be maintained by the use of uniforms, membership cards, or insignias. On the other hand, when the in-group develops around some kind of temporary activity (such as an organized hike through a state park), the boundaries that distinguish members from nonmembers are likely to be very informal.

Social Distance

Social distance signifies the degree to which people have a feeling of closeness or acceptance toward members of other groups. Most often, social distance is used to measure the degree of intimacy possible in social relationships among members of different racial and ethnic groups. Two persons may be physically close, yet not feel socially close, because they are members of different racial, ethnic, or age groups. Social distance is empirically measured by the use of self-report questionnaires or by observational techniques. A sociologist might measure social distance between political groups, social classes, religious groups, age groups, racial groups, or occupational groups.

Reference Groups

A reference group is a group that serves as a model when making evaluations and judgments about oneself. The group need not be one to which an individual belongs, but it is looked to as a standard of behavior, performance, values, or physical appearance. For example, a teenage girl may judge her appearance against that of actresses she sees in the movies or on TV, whether or not she aspires to an acting career.

Primary and Secondary Groups

Groups can also be characterized as either primary or secondary.

The Primary Group

The basic characteristics of the primary group include direct, intimate, face-to-face contact among members; strong emotional ties; permanence; endurance; and strong bonds of affection. Primary groups function as agents of socialization and social control. They provide the individual with emotional response and affection, contribute to the formation of the individual's personality and self-image, and provide the individual with security during times of stress and conflict. Primary groups are also cohesive because of the mutual bonds of affection that exist among members. The members have a sense that they belong together and have a feeling of common identity. The family is a primary group because it socializes the individual, is an important agent of social control, and provides each member with emotional support and love. The family is no longer a primary group if its members cease to interact with one another or if they fail to meet each other's emotional needs. Furthermore, the family is not labeled a primary group if it is characterized by habitual conflict or if its members fail to derive satisfaction from one another's presence.

Other examples of the primary group may be found in small clubs and among members of primitive hunting and gathering societies.

The Secondary Group

Secondary groups are utilitarian; the members get together because they have a job to do, and not necessarily because they value each other's presence. Once the job is done, secondary groups tend to disperse. Unlike members of a primary group, individuals in a secondary group do not help satisfy one another's needs for support, intimacy, or affection. The military, large bureaucratic corporations, and bureaus of federal and state governments are examples of secondary groups. In such groups, highly structured roles, laws, and contracts define responsibilities of the members. Although secondary groups tend to be large, smaller primary groups can usually be identified within them. For example, workers in large organizations often form cliques. Clique members have similar attitudes, values, and interests and feel that they need one another's companionship.

Gemeinschaft and Gesellschaft

The German sociologist Ferdinand Tonnies[1] developed the concepts of *Gemeinschaft* and *Gesellschaft* to denote two different kinds of social relationships in groups. The *Gemeinschaft* may be viewed as analogous to the primary group and the *Gesellschaft* as analogous to the secondary group. In general terms, *Gemeinschaft* represents social relationships in a community, and *Gesellschaft* represents social relationships in a society. The *Gemeinschaft* relationship is characterized by close, intimate, interpersonal ties; genuine concern with each other's welfare; and mutual trust and cooperation. The *Gesellschaft* relationship is characterized by competition, self-interest, efficiency, progress, and specialization.

Trend Toward Secondary-Group Association

Tonnies believed that as the urbanization of society increased, there would be a corresponding increase in *Gesellschaft* relationships. As he predicted, increasing industrialization and urbanization have necessitated more secondary group relationships. The resulting mobility and

---

1   Tonnies, Ferdinand, *Community and Society* (1887), trans. and ed. by Charles A. Loomis, (East Lansing: The Michigan State University Press, 1957).

changing family patterns have weakened primary groups and made them transient, thus depriving individuals of the stability they once experienced. The advantage of the *Gesellschaft* is that it has contributed to the strengthening of secondary groups, for with the *Gesellschaft* came an increased level of organizational efficiency, the development of individual talents through specialization, and the replacement of primary group provincialism.

For example, modern advances in medicine, which have had a direct effect on increasing life expectancy, would not have been possible without the ability of the physician to specialize in a particular field. The bureaucratic departmentalized structure of hospitals, the development of governmental agencies that generate research funds and monitor results, and a rapid system of mass communication operated by huge corporations have all contributed to medical progress. The rural family doctor simply does not have the resources available that now exist within the large health institutions, with their bureaucratic super-structure and secondary relationships.

Although secondary groups have gained in importance, primary groups remain a most significant element in society. The family, for instance, a crucial primary group, is still the major source of satisfaction of the human need for intimate affectionate relationships.

Therapeutic and Encounter Groups

Therapeutic groups are those in which people come together to find compassion and mutual support in an attempt to deal with a common problem or issue. Such groups may involve alcoholics, smokers, the overweight, the physically handicapped, and so on.

Encounter groups are made up of people with many different kinds of needs who direct their attention to increased emotional and attitudinal learning. Their goal is to understand themselves with increased objectivity, to heighten their self-awareness and their sense of mutual trust, and thus to feel more comfortable when interacting with others. The members of encounter groups express their emotions toward one another both physically and verbally.

Group Structure

All groups have structure. Group structure is the patterned relationships and opportunities for communication among members in a group. The relationships among the members of a group may take many forms, ranging from the formal to the informal.

Formal Structure

The formal structure of a group is represented by the recognized rules, regulations, and conditions that determine the roles and activities of its members. When formal structure is examined, one often finds such documents as bylaws, constitutions, statutes, and organizational charts outlining the chain of command.

The following characteristics are associated with formally structured groups:

1. Established patterns of communication

2. Formal application of discipline

3. Assignment of specialized tasks and responsibilities

4. Recognized chain of authority

5. Application of predetermined positive and negative sanctions used to reward and punish group members

The one great weakness of a formal structure is that the structure often becomes more important than the goals for which the structure exists.

An example of a group with formally structured member relationships is a large university system. The university structure contains statutes that spell out the goals, objectives, regulations, and organization of the university. A board of directors has either been appointed or elected for a specific period of time because the statutes dictate that this must be done. The president is the chief administrative officer because the statutes demand that such an office be occupied. Faculty are promoted and awarded tenure or are terminated because they have met or failed to meet standards expected of them. In sum, the members of a university function under a formal structure, operating according to a chain of command, with the roles, authority, and responsibilities of each member clearly defined and documented.

Informal Structure

A group can also perform with an informal structure, which consists of those spontaneous relationships that develop among the group members. The members have their own leaders and develop an unwritten code of behavior to which they adhere.

Disadvantages of an informal group structure are a lack of specified or uniform decision standards and more opportunity for bias in decisions. For example, if a large university had unwritten codes rather than formal statutes that spelled out the rules and regulations for faculty promotion, then promotion decisions would be unspecified and biased.

One of the advantages of an informal structure is that it gives people the flexibility to adapt to changing conditions without waiting for the formal processes of the group to be set into motion. Even within a large formally structured group, informal groups may develop as members get to know one another and form personal relationships. Through this informal structure, procedures may emerge that will allow people to solve problems not being adequately covered by formal regulations.

For example, when members of a local police department are engaged in contract negotiations with a municipality, they may, as a strategy, obey and enforce all rules and regulations in order to both create a work slowdown and make their presence (and problems) known to local residents. To accomplish this goal, they may issue traffic tickets to drivers whose infractions would ordinarily go unnoticed. In addition, they may stop large numbers of drivers in order to conduct safety inspections of their vehicles. The police officers' hope is that the local residents will soon be "fed up" with these actions and demand that the city settle on a contract. Thus, by organizing informally, the police officers can carry out a campaign that will expedite the signing of the formal contract.

Types of Leaders

A leader is a member of the group who is in a position to influence and direct the behavior of others. Sociologists distinguish two types of leaders: the task leader and the socio-emotional leader.

1. The *task leader* is the person who organizes and directs the group, keeping in mind the group's goals and objectives and formulating the means used to reach them.

2. The *socio-emotional leader* is the person who creates feelings of good will and harmony within the group and therefore is usually liked by all members.

In problem-solving groups, these two types of leaders emerge, although sometimes one person can perform both tasks.

Styles of Leadership

Sociologists also recognize three distinct styles of leadership:

1. The *authoritarian leader* makes all decisions that affect the group and simply orders others to carry out these decisions.

2. The *democratic leader* looks to the group for the development of ideas and proposals in order to accomplish the goals of the group. Here, decision-making is based on group consensus.

3. The *laissez-faire leader* usually has other interests and a hands-off approach toward directing group activities and goals. These leaders are extremely passive, and the direction that the group takes is not their main priority.

CHAPTER 8

Social Institutions and Formal Organizations

Sociologists distinguish between social institutions and formal and informal organizations. This chapter takes a close look at both. Social institutions are systems of norms, values, and structures that help a society identify and meet certain goals. These goals are broadly defined, and the values they embody are central to a society's way of life. Formal organizations, on the other hand, are actual groups of people, rather than systems of norms and values, who coordinate their efforts to achieve some very clearly defined goal. The formal organization tends to be large; it is characterized by specific rules and regulations and by a hierarchy of authority and responsibility. The United States Army, General Motors, the Chase Manhattan Bank, and the University of Wisconsin are examples of formal organizations. The informal organization is generally smaller, has less clearly defined goals, and does not depend on a rather rigid set of rules and procedures in going about its business. An amateur singing society, a group of one's friends, and a neighborhood association of homeowners are likely to be informal in their organization.

Social Institutions

An institution is a relatively permanent, organized system of social patterns that embodies certain sanctioned and unified behaviors for the purpose of satisfying and meeting the basic needs of a society. Five basic social institutions are found in all societies: the familial, educational, religious, economic, and governmental institutions. Each institution has certain functions and responsibilities.

Characteristics of Institutions

Following are six of the more important characteristics of institutions:

1. Each institution has as its primary objective the satisfaction of specific social needs. To satisfy these needs, each institution has multiple functions to perform. For instance, the family is responsible for controlling reproduction, socializing children, and providing economic security for its members. The government is responsible for maintaining order within a society, defending the society against outside attacks, and establishing rules or laws.

2. Institutions embody the ultimate values that are shared by their members. In the United States, the values found within the governmental institution include a democratic system of running the affairs of state, open elections, a representative legislative branch, and equality before the law.

3. Institutions are relatively permanent, in that the behavioral patterns established within the institutions become part of the tradition of the given culture. In Western countries, there is a strong tradition of monogamy (one man married to one woman). In addition, the members of a family all occupy an assigned role and status that is based on the age and the sex of each member.

4. The social bases of institutions are so broad that their activities occupy a central place within a society; a dramatic change in one institution is likely to produce changes in the others. For example, all institutions within a society are influenced by severe fluctuations in

the economic cycle. Periods of inflation, recession, and depression will not only affect one's job, but they may also have a profound influence on the stability of the family, the quality of education, and the ability of the government to provide necessary services to the people.

5. Even though all institutions are interdependent within a society, each individual institution is highly structured and organized around an expected set of norms, values, statuses, rules, groups, organizations, and behavioral patterns. Educational institutions, for example, contain school systems, teachers, administrators, etc., and have become extremely bureaucratic. There is a high value placed on learning and the accumulation of knowledge, earning high grades, progressing from one class to the next, developing good study habits, and cooperating with both teachers and fellow students.

6. The ideals of an institution are generally accepted by the great majority of the members of a society, regardless of whether or not they actually participate in the institution. For example, a bachelor, even though he chooses to remain apart from the traditional family structure, would not necessarily disagree with the function that the family serves in society.

Institutional Traits

There are also numerous traits that are associated with institutions. These traits are the smallest units of an institution. The most common of these traits may be placed into three distinct categories: cultural symbols, codes of behavior, and ideology.

Cultural Symbols

Cultural symbols are identifying signs or reminders of the presence of an institution. The symbols may be either material or nonmaterial. The flag, a national anthem, the crucifix, the Jewish star, a cathedral, and a logo are all cultural symbols that serve as reminders of specific social institutions.

Codes of Behavior

Codes of behavior are formal rules of conduct and informal traditions appropriate to certain roles. Although commonly shared codes of behavior exist, there is no guarantee that individuals will not deviate from them. If a person is to function effectively in an institutional role, he/she must be properly socialized into that role. For example, the majority of doctors who take the Hippocratic Oath, the ethical code of the medical profession, abide by it, but there are some doctors who will deviate and engage in unethical medical practices.

Ideology

Ideology is a system of interdependent ideas that is shared by a group. An ideology justifies a particular social, moral, economic, or political interest of a group, explaining the universe in terms that are acceptable to it. For example, the political ideology in the United States centers upon a fundamental belief in democracy. In the Jewish religion, the shared ideology is an acceptance of Judaism.

Institutionalization

Institutionalization is the development of a regular system of circumscribed norms, statuses, and roles that are accepted by the society. Through institutionalization, spontaneous and unpredictable behavior is replaced with behavior that is regular and predictable.

For example, within the government, each participant has a role to play and a set of rules to follow. Most people are simply citizens who play an active role in terms of electing their representatives. Other people, however, have more specialized roles, such as congresswoman, assemblyman, mayor, governor, senator, and police commissioner. Because the behavior of each of these public servants is governed by codes, statutes, regulations, and court decisions, it is fairly easy to predict what course of action each might take under a given set of circumstances. When institutionalization does not occur for members of a particular social position in society, specific guidelines for appropriate behavior in that role are lacking. This situation can create confusion for the members of that social group as well as for those outside it.

Functions of Institutions

Sociologists have found it useful to distinguish between the manifest and the latent functions of institutions. They also recognize the basic functions common to all institutions and the more specific functions characteristic of each separate institution.

Manifest and Latent Functions

The manifest functions of institutions are those that are obvious, apparent, and generally accepted by the members of society. The latent functions of institutions are those that are less obvious and apparent, functions that may even be disapproved of by the members of society. For example, the manifest functions of a political party include selecting the candidates who best represent the ideals and goals of the party, are attractive to the voters, and will make a contribution to their office once elected. The latent functions of the political party, on the other hand, may include a strong system of patronage for giving jobs to those who have been loyal to the party, a method of protecting from prosecution those past members who have committed crimes, and a system for collecting funds from lobbyists and special-interest groups.

Basic Functions of Institutions

All institutions have the following basic functions:

1. Institutions provide for the individual a model of appropriate social behavior in various situations. Through the socialization process (see Chapter 4), the socially acceptable and socially unacceptable ways of behaving are passed on to the individual. For example, when voting in a public election, we know that we should be legally registered in the right precinct, that we wait in line until it is our turn, that we close the curtain when entering the booth, and that we vote only once.

2. Institutions provide a large number of roles and define appropriate role behavior for individuals. A person can decide which role(s) he/she will best fit, because he/she can learn the expectations of a particular role before actually assuming that role (anticipatory socialization). For example, we have the opportunity to witness the role behavior of lawyers, doctors, accountants, professors, and other

occupations. An individual can determine a suitable occupation by evaluating these role behaviors and learning about their educational requirements.

3. Institutions serve the culture by providing its members with stability and consistency. We tend to think of the institutionalized way as the proper way of behaving. For example, churchgoers accept many of the values and beliefs of the religious institution to which they belong.

4. Institutions tend to both regulate and control behavior because they embody the accepted expectations of society. Negative sanctions (punishment and ridicule) are set up as deterrents for those who do not conform. For example, for a person without money, committing a robbery may be an unacceptable alternative because it is likely to result in apprehension, conviction, and a prison sentence. Rather than risk punishment, the person registers at the unemployment office, collects welfare, or even accepts private charity.

Specialized Functions of Institutions

Each of the five social institutions listed below exists for a specific purpose and performs certain specialized functions.

The Family

1. Regulation of sexual behavior

2. Replacement of members from generation to generation through reproduction

3. Care and protection of children, the infirm, and the elderly

4. Socialization of children

5. Fixing social placement and establishing status, passed on through social inheritance

6. Economic security provided by the family as the basic unit of economic production and consumption

Educational Institutions

1. Providing preparation for occupational roles

2. Serving as a vehicle for the transmission of cultural heritage

3. Acquainting individuals with various roles in society

4. Preparing individuals for certain expected social roles

5. Promoting change through involvement in scientific research

6. Strengthening personal adjustment and improving social relationships

Religious Institutions

1. Assistance in the search for moral identity

2. Providing interpretations to help explain one's physical and social environment

3. Promotion of sociability, social cohesion, and group solidarity

Economic Institutions

1. Production of goods and services

2. Distribution of goods and services along with distribution of economic resources (labor and equipment)

3. Consumption of goods and services

Governmental Institutions

1. The institutionalization of norms through laws or rules passed by the legislative bodies of government

2. The enforcement of laws that have been passed

3. Resolution of conflicts existing among members of society

4. Establishment of services such as health care, education, welfare, and so on

5. Protection of citizens from attack by other nations and maintenance of civil alertness to danger

Relationships Among Institutions

In terms of the functions that they perform, the five basic social institutions are highly related. If a society is to function effectively, the basic institutions must relate to one another in an efficient and productive manner. A proper and sometimes delicate balance must be maintained between the familial, governmental, religious, economic, and educational institutions. Because institutions perform numerous functions that sometimes overlap, it is at times difficult to hold this balance in place. Although several institutions may be capable of contributing to a similar need, it is inevitable that a single institution will remain dominant and exercise considerable influence over the others. For example, both the family and the formal educational institutions contribute to the socialization of young people. In a modern industrial society, the schools have the primary responsibility for performing the educational function. In rural agricultural communities, however, the family does a good deal of the educating, since the expectation may be that the children will one day assume the responsibilities of running the family farm.

Transfer of Functions

As certain institutions gain in importance, there will be a shifting of specific institutional functions from one institution to another. Such a shift in function may take place when either one of two conditions exists: (1) an institution fails to meet a given need, or (2) two or more institutions are capable of meeting the need, but one clearly demonstrates that it can perform at a superior level. For example, in modern industrial society, the family has probably lost more functions than any other institution. Most of the socialization function has been assumed by the schools. Furthermore, the family unit is now primarily a consumer of goods (while at one time it was both a producer and a consumer), and the economic factors that affect the family are now controlled by the economic institutions and government.

Competition Among Institutions

There is a strong element of competition among institutions that may eventually lead to the weakening of one or more elements within an institution. This competitive spirit exists because each institution, by performing a variety of essential functions, enters into competition with other institutions that may perform the same functions.

Certain institutions may exert considerable influence over others. For example, in the United States, government exerts a good deal of influence over the other four social institutions. Even in its relationship with religious institutions, the government, through the legislature and the court system, makes certain decisions that affect the tax-exempt status of church income and property.

Cooperation Among Institutions

For institutions to be collectively effective, they must support and depend upon one another. An appropriate example is the close relationship between the educational system and political institutions. Since a very large part of our educational system lies in the public sector, educational institutions are closely related to political institutions, especially units of state and local government.

Furthermore, as changes take place within one institution, there are usually corresponding changes taking place in other institutions as well. Therefore, when functions are gained or lost in a particular institution, internal adjustments must be made so that the institution can either provide the new service or concentrate on its remaining functions. When the United States went to war in 1941, not only were there changes in government in terms of priorities and services rendered, but there were also changes in the economic institutions (retooling for wartime production), the family (women entered the labor market), and the schools (curricula were modified to place an emphasis on wartime needs).

Institutional Universality and Variation

The basic needs of people in every society must be satisfied in a manner that is culturally approved and accepted by its members. The five basic social institutions are present in some form, no matter how primitive or advanced a society. There is, however, tremendous variation in the way these needs are met. A particular behavior pattern may be more beneficial to the members of one society than it is to another. Because societies are at different levels of development, they have different degrees of knowledge and technology, each of which is more or less conducive to certain types of behavior patterns. Institutions differ, therefore, from one culture to another because there are many different ways in which tasks can be carried out. The patterns of family life, the religious doctrine, the method of socialization, the economic system, and the form of government will change as we move from one culture to the next. In sum, the institutions themselves, and the characteristics and traits of institutions, are universal, but the functions institutions provide and the manner in which social needs are met vary from culture to culture.

Formal Organizations

Formal organizations are groups of people who have been brought together to achieve a specific purpose. They may be highly organized or loosely organized. The primary difference between a highly structured and a loosely structured organization is the amount of individual autonomy that members have in the organization. In the prototypical highly structured formal organization, members must obey the standing rules, with no deviation permitted. These rules are enforced by a small hierarchy of officials. Members of loosely structured formal organizations have considerably more autonomy. Leadership is less centralized, and the majority of the membership contributes to the decision-making process. Regulations are less narrowly defined, and individuals are allowed to adjust a broad set of regulations to individual situations.

Formal Organizations and Bureaucracy

A bureaucracy is a hierarchy of authority and responsibility that a formal organization may use to coordinate its activities and achieve its specialized goals. The formal organization is the group, whereas the bureaucracy is the mechanism used by the group to reach its goals. In a bureaucracy, all of the roles for the participating members are carefully planned so that the specialized goals can effectively be achieved.

As an organization grows, at some point a bureaucratic structure will emerge. General Motors, for example, is a formal organization that exists for the purpose of manufacturing automobiles and selling them at a profit. To accomplish these goals, the company has set up a bureaucracy that operates in an efficient and effective manner.

Characteristics of Bureaucracy

The sociologist Max Weber[1] believed that bureaucracy was more efficient than other forms of organization and could accomplish its goals with the maximum utilization of employees and a minimum of personal tension and friction. He also noted that, ideally, bureaucracy was less wasteful of money and precious time. Weber identified five major characteristics of a bureaucracy: specialization, hierarchy of authority, impersonal treatment, universal standards and qualifications, and written rules and regulations. These characteristics refer to an ideal model of bureaucracy conceived of by Weber; they do not always appear together in actual bureaucratic formal organizations.

Specialization

In a bureaucracy each person performs a narrowly defined task that is assigned to him/her. There is a greater need for specialization in bureaucratic organizations than in other forms of organization. For example, a worker on an automobile assembly line at General Motors may be assigned the single task of placing a chrome strip on the front fender as each new car passes by. In order for the organizational goal to be accomplished (in this case, production of cars), all workers must specialize at their tasks. Such division of labor is advantageous because it enables an organization to train individuals to carry out only one task or one particular aspect of a task. Tasks can then be performed quickly and efficiently. However, tasks may be so narrowly defined that the work becomes boring and repetitious.

Hierarchy of Authority

Each position in the organizational hierarchy carries with it specific responsibilities and duties (as well as privileges), and the individual must report to the person immediately above him/her in the hierarchy. All large organizations have a chain of command to which individuals must adhere. Authority in a bureaucracy rests in the office and not in the specific individual occupying that office. Formal organizations have so many employees that it would be impossible for one or a few super-

---

1   Max Weber, *Essays in Sociology* (1904), trans. and ed. by Talcott Parsons (New York: Charles Scribner's Sons, 1956).

visors to monitor all individuals who are performing tasks. If the organization gives certain groups of people the authority to supervise others, the organization will ensure that its work will be done effectively.

Impersonal Treatment

Social relationships between employees in a bureaucracy are analogous to secondary group social relationships; they are impersonal, consist of few face-to-face interactions, and lack emotional closeness. Workers within a bureaucracy are dealt with by the organization in accordance with the position that they hold rather than on a personal level. Impersonality is considered necessary because if individuals become involved in one another's personal problems, work will not be done effectively. Ideally, all workers who occupy a specific position or status are treated in the same manner. Within our government's civil service system, for example, all workers at a given level receive the same number of sick days off, the same number of vacation days, and the same salary.

Universalistic Standards and Qualifications

Personnel are not hired by a bureaucratic organization unless they meet the minimum qualifications for the position to which they are applying. These standards attempt to protect the worker from unjust treatment in hiring or promotion decisions. The federal government, for example, publishes the requirements for appointment to specific governmental positions along with the requirements for promotion. These requirements are followed to the letter. Applicants must have a combination of a minimum level of education, an acceptable score on a civil service examination, and a certain number of years of experience.

Written Rules and Regulations

The activities of the organization and of the workers therein are governed by an explicit set of rules and regulations. Rules and regulations ensure that the activities of the workers can be coordinated. Without these formal rules, individuals would be unclear as to the specific nature of their tasks. Furthermore, when an individual worker is replaced, the new worker can carry out the work in the same manner as in the past. Again, using governmental units as an example, the goals of each unit, the administration of the unit, and the rules governing its operation are spelled out in detail. All situations that arise should ideally be covered by the rules and regulations.

Informality in Formal Organizations

Weber identified important characteristics in the formal structure of organization but neglected to point out the informal characteristics. The formal or planned structure of an organization encompasses rules and regulations that its members must obey and specifies the roles they are expected to carry out. The informal structure of an organization refers to those aspects that are unplanned. It encompasses the unofficial rules that the members adhere to and the personal relationships that develop among members. Informal structure is important because it determines how the members will interact with each other and how they will respond to the official rules and regulations.

Furthermore, the members of the organization have personal and emotional needs that are not met by the impersonal formal structure. Workers need the emotional support and friendship that cliques and informal communication networks provide. They may want to make decisions about the way in which the work is carried out. They may also want to find out what is occurring within the organization and may do so through their own chain of communication. By allowing this informal structure to exist, the organization lets the workers meet these personal needs and desires.

The Development of Oligarchy

Rule by a few tends to develop in all formal organizations, even those opposed to such control. Oligarchy exists when a small clique of individuals who occupy the highest positions in the organization take responsibility for all the decision making. The "iron law of oligarchy," as it was called by Robert Michels,[2] states that it is inevitable that a small group will rule over an organization and will maintain its elite position for as long as possible. Michels believed that it was impossible

2   Robert Michels, *Political Parties: A Sociological Study of the Oligarchical Tendencies in Modern Democracy* (New York: The Free Press, 1949).

for large numbers of people to coordinate their own activities and rule themselves. He saw the majority of the population as being apathetic and too involved in their own affairs to be concerned with the business of leadership. Once a small number of people gain experience in leadership, the other members of the population become dependent on their knowledge and skills. Thus, the same small group continues to retain authority.

Problems of Bureaucratic Organizations

It is quite common to find discontent with bureaucratic rules and functioning among both members of the organization and their clients. Some of the problems that may arise in a bureaucratic organization are the development of a bureaucratic personality, ritualism, goal displacement, and conflict with professional ethics.

Bureaucratic Personality

Workers who have a bureaucratic personality are often inflexible and unable to adapt to novel situations. Without a written set of rules, it is difficult for them to react to a given problem; regardless of what happens, the written rules are followed to the letter.

Ritualism

Ritualism is the blind following of the rules of an organization without questioning whether these rules are beneficial and with no understanding of why the rules are being followed. In pure ritualism, the method of performing according to the rules is more important than accomplishing a goal. Adherence to ritualism often prevents innovations and hinders efficient completion of a task.

Goal Displacement

Sometimes the individuals who work within a bureaucracy lose sight of their organization's goals and replace them with their own goals, such as maintaining their status in the organization or avoiding work and responsibility. This is referred to as goal displacement.

Professional Ethics

Very often, professionals consider loyalty to their profession to be more important than loyalty to the organization in which they work. The ethical guidelines of their profession may sometimes contradict the rules and regulations of their employer.

Organizational Change

Changes may occur in an organization as a result of competition from other organizations, new technological developments, pressure from special-interest groups, changing economic conditions, or changes in the interests or values of the population. For example, as an organization, local government is subject to all of the above conditions. If the government cannot meet the needs of its constituents or respond to new technologies and economic changes, it may be replaced. Governmental officials may be replaced, singularly or collectively, when they repeatedly or seriously fail to respond to important changes.

CHAPTER 9

Marriage and the Family

The family is a basic social institution found in all societies. All families are embedded in larger networks known as kinship networks, which consist of individuals who are related by blood, marriage, or adoption. Patterns of marriage and the process of mate selection differ from culture to culture. However, whatever the culture, with marriage comes a new social role for the individual, along with certain expectations regarding behavior, attitudes, privileges, and obligations.

This chapter discusses the nature, function, and changing patterns of the family and its related structures. The last few decades have brought striking changes to the American family. Individuals are having earlier sexual experiences but getting married at a later age, adolescent pregnancies have doubled, divorce rates and single-parent families have increased, and the percentage of couples who choose to cohabit (live together, unmarried) is growing rapidly. With these changes in family structure and pattern have come changes in the functions families serve for both the individual and society.

The Family

The family may be thought of as an organized pattern of social relationships. Defining the word "family" is difficult because it is used to describe so many different patterns of relationships, such as one individual living with his/her children, a married man and woman with children, a married man and woman without children, an unmarried couple living with children, and a married man and women living with their children, parents, aunts, and uncles.

The family is a kinship group that has primary responsibility for the socialization of its children and the fulfillment of certain other basic needs. Unlike other social institutions, however (e.g., religious and economic institutions), the family can be defined as both a biological and a social group within society. It consists of a relatively permanent group of people who are embedded in an organized system of social relationships; are related to one another by blood, marriage, or adoption; and who live together for an indefinite period of time. An individual can be biologically related to other members of his/her family or can be related by some socioculturally defined ceremony such as marriage, adoption, or social categorization. In most Western societies, the members of a family usually collaborate financially and share responsibility in the socializing of children (if present).

Types of Families

The family exists in several different forms.

Nuclear Family

The nuclear family, also referred to as the "conjugal" family, is the basic family unit of husband, wife, and their offspring. Americans tend to see this form as an ideal type, being rather ethnocentric about its virtues and disregarding its limitations.

Extended Family

The extended family, sometimes also referred to as the "consanguine" family, is composed of more than two generations of family members. It is based upon the biological and social relationships of a large number of people, including parents, children, grandparents, uncles, aunts, and cousins. The extended family is more prevalent in societies or segments of society that face economic hardships. In such societies, the family members must work together and assist one another in order to survive, even to the extent of sharing economic resources and food.

Single-Parent Family

The single-parent family is one in which one parent is living with his/her offspring, either because of divorce, the death of one parent, single status adoption, or planned pregnancy. The proportion of single-parent families has recently increased in the United States. The term "single-parent family" is used even in cases of divorce where the other (noncustodial) parent plays an active role in the rearing of the children. Some sociologists suggest that such families be called "single-custody families."

Reconstituted (or Blended) Family

The reconstituted or blended family is a family formed by the remarriage of a parent following divorce or the death of the children's parent. These blended families, particularly those in which both individuals have children from a previous marriage, embrace new challenges for both the parents and the children. For example, parents may still have ties to ex-spouses; a parent may be making child support or alimony payments to another household; and the children may now have two natural parents but be living with one natural parent and a stepparent.

Cohabitation

In the United States, the unmarried couple who is childless and living together (cohabiting) is a social relationship that is becoming more common. Cohabitation, while prevalent in all age groups, seems to be the most popular among college-age individuals and senior citizens. Cohabitation usually refers to unmarried adults who are living together and presumably having a sexual relationship with one another. They may cohabit for an indefinite period of time, share financial responsibilities, and eventually bear and rear children together.

The U.S. Census Bureau, however, does not consider the cohabiting couple a family, but categorizes it separately as a POSSLQ: persons of the opposite sex sharing living quarters. There has been much criticism of this category. First, the definition does not specify that the two persons who are living together have a sexual relationship with one another; a POSSLQ may include households where males and females live together but are just platonic roommates. Second, it fails to include persons of the same sex living together. Third, it does not indicate how long a couple must live together to qualify.

Kinship

Kinship refers to a rather large network of people who are related to each other by common ancestry, by marriage, or by adoption. Through the system of kinship we are able to organize and identify relationships that exist within families. Because American society has demonstrated a rather strong commitment to the nuclear family type, the larger kinship group to which a person belongs has lost a good deal of its importance. We tend to see our "distant" relatives only on special occasions such as holidays and celebrations. If asked what our second cousin's occupation is or where this cousin lives, we may be hard-pressed to answer.

Functions of the Family

As pointed out in Chapter 8, all social institutions have as an objective the satisfaction of specific social needs within society. As a social institution, the family performs many functions, the nature of which and their level of performance vary from society to society. The specific functions of the family in the United States, first mentioned in Chapter 8, will be examined here in greater detail.

Care and Protection of the Children, the Infirm, and the Elderly

In Western societies, the family has traditionally been responsible for the psychological, physical, and economic care of its children since children are incapable of assuming these functions on their own. Thus, the family makes sure that its members have food, shelter, and protection from outside forces. The family also provides individuals with a sense of belonging, affection, and emotional support. In addition, the family has traditionally been responsible for taking care of and comforting the infirm and providing economic security for the elderly.

Socialization of Children

Throughout human history, the family has been the primary agency for the initial socialization of the young. For a significant period of time after birth, the family is the only group with which the child has extensive contact. Thus, the family plays a major role in shaping the attitudes, values, and beliefs of the child and in influencing the kind of relationships that he/she will develop with other social agencies and institutions. It is the family that prepares the child for taking on the social role of a member of the society in which he/she lives.

Fixing Social Placement and Establishing Status

Every known society uses a system of rules of descent to determine the proper social placement and status of a child, and to identify the relatives and the family to which a person belongs. Inheritance and power relationships in families are also determined by rules of descent. The family traditionally confers an ascribed status on each of its members. Although individuals can move from one social class to another, each person initially lives within the social class of his/her family. This initial family social class influences the subsequent social class of the individual in two ways. Since the socialization process is such a basic and important cultural function of the family, the process itself naturally prepares family members for a continued life within the same social class. In addition, in every class-oriented society, one's social class of origin limits the opportunities that are available and consequently, one's ability to move from class to class.

Regulation of Sexual Activities

The family has traditionally been responsible for the regulation of sexuality as well as for the replacement of members through reproduction. It regulates sexuality by providing morals and values regarding what the society considers appropriate sexual behavior and appropriate sexual partners. Societal practices range from strictly prohibiting and penalizing sexual relationships except among married couples, to those that encourage premarital or extramarital sexual relationships.

The incest taboo, which is found in almost every society, regulates sexuality by requiring individuals to choose sexual partners outside of the family rather than from among family members. This taboo exists for both biological and social reasons. First, it prevents biological inbreeding, which may cause genetic deformities in the offspring. Second, it preserves social identities, roles, and authority within families. Third, it allows individuals to bond emotionally and socially to many people, not to just a few members of the same primary group. When individuals marry, assuming that they don't marry within their family, the union will bring together unrelated families.

Marriage

Marriage is the culturally approved social relationship for sexual relationships and childbearing. Many cultures accept sexual relationships (premarital, extramarital, and homosexual behavior) outside of marriage, but most cultures discourage the bearing and rearing of children outside of marriage. This insistence on a marital framework is designed to protect children; children should have kinship networks to take care of them both financially and socially. Although this cultural norm persists in American society, it is fairly common for children to be born or reared outside of marriage, such as in the cases of unwanted teenage pregnancies, unmarried women choosing voluntary pregnancy by artificial insemination, the use of surrogate mothers, and homosexual partners (legally unmarried) adopting children. These particular situations, however, are not fully approved by society.

When an individual marries, he/she acquires another social role (husband, wife), along with identified expectations regarding behavior, attitudes, privileges, and obligations. It is acknowledged by others in the society that he/she is now beginning a family. In general sociological terms, therefore, marriage is the acquisition of a new social role, and the recognition of this new status by others.

Types of Marriage Patterns

Marriage patterns vary from culture to culture.

Monogamy

Monogamy is the marriage of one woman and one man at a time. The most widely practiced form of marriage, this is the type practiced in the Western world. All U.S. states have legal prohibitions against an individual's having more than one spouse. The penalties for deviating from these laws can be severe.

Polygamy

Polygamy is the marriage of a person of either sex to more than one spouse. In the past, polygamy was the preferred form of marriage around the world. In some societies where polygamy is practiced, having more than one spouse serves as a status symbol.

There are two forms of polygamy:

Polygyny is the marriage of one man to more than one woman.

Polyandry, which is less common, is the marriage of one woman to more than one man.

The economic conditions of a society are related to the number of polygamous marriages in that society. For example, in some societies having more than one wife is an economic or social advantage, and the man who achieves this will enjoy high status. Polygyny exists where males can afford to support two or more wives. On the other hand, polyandry has been found in societies with severe economic hardships (through polyandry, family size is limited).

Group Marriage

Group marriage is a form of marriage in which two or more men are living with two or more women at the same time. Today there is no known society where group marriage has been institutionalized as the accepted form.

Mate Selection

Societies have different ways of bringing couples together in marriage. Wives may be purchased through the exchange of gifts or a direct monetary payment. In some cultures there is a practice known as wife capture. Marriages can also be arranged by one's parents or other close relatives; in this method, mate selection becomes a prerogative of the family, with or without the consent of the children involved.

In the United States, marriages are formed by the free choice of both parties. Although most Americans believe that they have complete freedom to pick whomever they wish as their mates, there are restrictions that influence their choices. These constraints may not be as formal as family arrangements, but they limit the individuals that are eligible and available to a particular person. The mate selection process is, in fact, influenced by a variety of structural, cultural, and interpersonal factors.

Informal Influences of Family and Peers

To a great extent, parents determine what potential partners their children will be exposed to by living in a particular neighborhood and sending their children to a certain type of educational institution. Children learn from their parents and peers what qualities to look for in a marriage partner. The feelings, attitudes, and prejudices of one's family and friends largely influence one's choice.

Limiting Rules of Society

In many societies, social norms dictate the type of person with whom we can or cannot have a relationship. Two of the most common are the rules of endogamy and exogamy.

Endogamy.   An endogamous rule specifies that the marriage partner be a member of a certain group, whether it be one of social class, religion, caste, race, or nationality. Even though in the United States there are few formal endogamous norms, there are a host of informal expectations that are held by one's family and friends. A person often feels extreme social pressure to marry within his/her race, age group, religion, and social class.

Exogamy.   Societies also have rules regarding who one should not marry. An exogamous rule specifies that the marriage partner be from outside a specified group. All societies are exogamous in that they forbid an individual to marry his/her close blood relatives. Individuals may be urged to marry outside their clan, village, tribe, or kinship group.

The Incest Taboo. The incest taboo, an extension of the exogamous rule, specifically forbids sexual relations between blood-related family members, such as siblings, grandparents and grandchildren, and parent and child. Except in certain rare circumstances, the incest taboo is found in almost every known society. If incest and marriage among blood relatives were a common practice, the family would cease to act as a functional unit where social roles are clearly defined. Family relationships, roles, and authority patterns would be greatly complicated and confused. For example, a female child produced by a mother-son union would be both a "sister" of the father and a "granddaughter" of the mother.

Social Context

Another important factor in mate selection is the social context within which interaction and selection take place. Propinquity, routine activities, and familiarity are all social contextual factors that influence with whom we come into contact, and the attitudes formed after these contacts.

Propinquity. Considering all the people there are in the world, we are of course more likely to meet and make contact with those individuals who are in close proximity to us, be they coworkers, neighbors in our apartment complex, or students sitting next to us in class.

Routine Activities. We are more likely to meet and strike up a conversation with persons in the social context of our routine activities. Routine activities provide us with topics of mutual interest with which to begin conversations. For example, a person who joins a wine-tasting club, which meets every week, has an available pool of others at the club who share a common interest. Furthermore, the person has a nice conversation opener: "What did you think of that burgundy we just tasted?"

Familiarity. According to the "mere exposure effect," continual interaction with another person produces positive attitudes toward that person. The more often you ride on the bus with a particular person, the more likely you are to be attracted to him/her.

Interpersonal Factors in Mate Selection

There are still other factors that reduce our potential field of eligible mates but have personal value for us. Those factors that motivate us to choose one partner over another in order to gain emotional satisfaction, good feelings, or self-esteem are physical attractiveness, similarity, and romantic love.

Physical Attractiveness

Physical attractiveness appears to be a major factor in the initial stages of interaction but decreases in importance as individuals get to know one another. People assume, men more than women, that by associating with physically attractive people they will be perceived more favorably themselves. Furthermore, people tend to attribute other desired qualities to a physically attractive person. For example, if a person is good-looking, it is assumed that he/she must also be nice, intelligent, and capable.

Similarity

People are attracted to and are more likely to marry others who are similar to them in attitudes, age, social class, race, ethnicity, and other personal characteristics. In more formal terms, this is referred to as the theory of *homogamy*. Similarity, especially with regard to attitudes, figures largely in selecting a mate because people who are like us reinforce our own attitudes and world views, and consequently, they give us feedback that what we think and feel is correct. We seek out similar people for another reason—since they are like us, they will probably like us in return.

Romantic Love

People also select marriage partners for emotional reasons. As a cultural trait, romantic love is found primarily in the Western industrial countries. To most Americans, romantic love is a natural prerequisite to marriage, but this value is by no means universally shared. Romantic love is functional in that it helps young people cut the ties to their families and provides the newly married couple with the affection and emotional support that they once received from their own families.

Theories of Mate Selection

The previous paragraphs have described factors that influence with whom we come into contact, to whom we are attracted, and whom we may choose as a marital partner. Process theorists assume that there is no one factor that determines whom we select as a mate, but instead, the process is influenced by many structural, cultural, and interpersonal factors. We screen persons, and based on certain disqualifications, we eliminate them from our pool of eligible mates. This filtering process occurs until a mate is chosen. There are, however, theories that attempt to explain mate selection in terms of one specific factor or process rather than as a combination of many factors.

Social Exchange Theory

Social exchange theory describes mate selection as a process where the individual "shops" for the right partner, similar to shopping for the right computer or refrigerator. Each of us has certain assets and liabilities to bring to a relationship. We choose partners based on what we have to offer and what they are able to give in return. According to social exchange theory, we desire an equal exchange in "goods."

Equity Theory

A variation of social exchange theory, equity theory emphasizes fairness in this mate selection comparison. We select partners who give us the same relative value as we give them. An equal exchange is not what is desired, but rather a perceived fair exchange. For example, a beautiful woman who goes out with an unattractive doctor may view the relationship as fair because she brings to it her beauty and in exchange receives a partner who is likely to make a lot of money. Equity theory holds that when an individual feels that he/she is giving more proportionately than he/she is receiving, or vice versa, this individual will not feel comfortable with the relationship, and therefore, it may not last.

Other Theories

Other theories that have attempted to explain the mate selection process include *Winch's*[1] *complementary needs theory*, where individuals choose partners that complement their personality needs; and *psychodynamic theory*, which states that individuals choose partners who satisfy emotional needs stemming from early familial and childhood experiences.

---

1   R. F. Winch, *The Modern Family* (New York: Holt, 1971).

Industrialization, Urbanization, and the Family

As society began to change from an agrarian to an industrial form, both the structure and the function of the family changed with it.

Weakening of Extended Kinship Ties

Perhaps the most significant result of the move away from the traditional rural family and toward the urban-industrial family was the shift from the extended kinship group to the dominant nuclear family. Ties to the extended family were weakened for three reasons:

1. The individual in an urban society had to be geographically mobile. Within an urban-industrial complex, an individual's promotion and the corresponding heightening of social status are achieved by recognized performance on the job. To be promoted, however, a person may have to be transferred to a different city. The nuclear family will usually remain together, but the extended family will be left behind.

2. Formal groups were substituted for traditional kin groups in helping people cope with their problems. A person who is in need of help in an urban society may very well seek assistance from a professional who is a stranger to him/her, rather than seek help from his/her extended family members.

3. Although initial status was still determined by the family, individuals now had an opportunity to achieve a desired status on their own.

Loss of Functions to Other Social Institutions

In society's move toward urbanization, the family lost many of its functions to other social institutions.

Loss of Socialization Function

As economic production moved from the family to the factory, it was necessary for the formal educational institutions to increase the role they played in socialization. Very often, preparation for work in an urban society required a high level of specialization that could only be offered by technical schools and universities.

Loss of Economic and Protective Functions

Many economic functions have also been removed from the family unit. In urbanized societies, as the family changed from being both a unit of production and consumption to primarily a unit of consumption, it was no longer necessary to have a large number of children and other relatives available for work. In the urban community, a family with many children to support was more apt to suffer financial hardships than was a smaller family. Furthermore, the government has come to play a major role in assuming financial responsibility (traditionally a function of just the family) for those who cannot provide for themselves— through federal social programs such as welfare, social security, public housing, and health assistance programs. Care of the seriously ill, the mentally and physically handicapped, and the dependent elderly has shifted from the family to the hospital, rehabilitation center, mental institution, and nursing home.

Gain in the Importance of Specific Functions

The affection, intimacy, and support that the family has traditionally provided is a function that has increased in importance with industrialization. Urban communities usually lack primary group ties with neighbors and other community members. People who live in high-rise apartments rarely know even the other people who live on their floors. Presently, the family has as an important objective the satisfaction of emotional and psychological needs.

Changes in Family Structure

Changes in the structure of the American family have been seen as the results of a decrease in family size, a shift in attitudes toward divorce, and modifications in the role of both women and men.

Decrease in Family Size

The decrease in family size is due to three main factors:

1. The change in the role of children that has accompanied the move

from a basically agrarian society to a largely urban industrialized one. Children in an urban industrial society become an economic burden rather than an asset to the family.

2. The increased level of education. Highly educated couples tend to have fewer children than do couples with limited education.

3. The widespread availability of birth control devices and counseling. This has given individuals the ability to choose how many children they will have, or even if they will have children at all.

Shift in Attitudes Toward Divorce

As divorce has become an accepted, respectable method of ending a marriage where children are involved, changes have taken place in the family. When a husband-father or wife-mother leaves the family household residence, the functions and responsibilities of the remaining family members must be adjusted to make up for the loss. Furthermore, most divorced individuals remarry, and blended or reconstituted families are formed. These blended families create new sets of problems and issues, such as finances, stepparenting, and the roles of in-laws and ex-spouses, with which family members must now deal.

Changes in Roles

The expectations and roles of both marriage partners have changed drastically since World War II, but the change has been most obvious for the female. In an increasing number of cases, the wife is now working, contributing to the family income and gaining authority within the family. Many middle-class women are now completing their education, getting married, and working until the first child is born, either caring for the child through infancy or bringing someone else into the home to do this so that the mother can return to a full-time career.

The women's liberation movement was very influential in changing these gender-role expectations within the family. In many marriages, men are becoming increasingly involved in domestic chores, while their wives are entering the labor market and contributing to the economic support of the household. The distribution of power is also becoming more egalitarian. However, despite these changes, the traditional gender roles for husband and wife are still the norm in most American families.

Divorce

Divorce has become more acceptable in American society over the past few decades. In the past, unhappily married couples would stay together because they felt it would be in the best interests of the children. However, there is now a realization that a home life characterized by conflict may be more harmful to a child than the divorce of the parents.

The fact that divorce rates have been significantly higher in mid-twentieth-century America than they were in prior years may be more a function of our changing society and values than a result of the breakdown and deterioration of the family as a social institution. The family continues to be of major importance in American society, even with the rising divorce rate. The rate of remarriage among those who have been divorced is high. Today, couples who are unhappy with their marriage need not stay together because of economic necessity, since their economic needs may be met by other institutions.

The possible reasons for the disruption of a marriage through divorce are almost endless because a marriage involves two individuals with unique personalities and differing backgrounds who come to live together. Nonetheless, sociologists have developed structural, cultural, and interpersonal explanations for why some marital relationships end in divorce.

Structural Factors in Divorce

Urban living and geographic mobility have had a significant impact on the family by reducing the kinds of functions that it once performed. Both husband and wife are no longer solely dependent on the family for the production of necessities and the delivery of services, which makes it much easier, practically speaking, to dissolve a marriage in an urban industrial environment than it was to dissolve a marriage in an agrarian society.

Economic factors in society have also played an important role. For example, general attitudes toward fulfillment for the individual and against group obligation, as well as changes in women's employment opportunities, have influenced individuals' assessments of the costs and benefits of staying in or leaving a marital relationship.

Cultural Factors in Divorce

The cultural stigma of divorce has lessened in urban industrial societies, particularly in the United States. Divorce has become a socially acceptable solution for a marriage that is not succeeding. This public sentiment has been supported in most states by changes in legislation pertaining to divorce and the restructuring of court procedures to move uncontested cases through swiftly.

Interpersonal/Relational Factors in Divorce

There are also interpersonal/relational factors in the dissolution of marriage.

Early Marriage

Teenaged couples who marry are more likely to divorce. These young people usually interrupt their education and therefore must work at lower-paying jobs, which places stress on their marriages. Teenaged couples may also marry under conditions of parental opposition and unwanted pregnancy. College-educated individuals are less likely to divorce because they marry later and are generally better off economically.

Length of Marriage

As the length of the marriage increases, couples are more likely to stay in it because they have invested both extrinsically (material goods, shared finances, children, friends) and intrinsically (self-disclosure, emotional effort, shared time and experiences) in the relationship.

High Expectations

One partner may have high expectations for the other prior to the marriage that are never fulfilled. These expectations may involve a couple's future social status, sexual relationship, popularity, good health, job security, and proper role as a spouse. To many Americans, romantic love is the most significant part of a marriage. Before marriage, a couple believes that if their love for one another does not fail, then any obstacle can be overcome. They soon realize that the magnitude of romantic love that they once enjoyed has now left them, and they have to resort to more practical means if their problems are to be solved.

Part IV:
Social Stratification

This section examines social stratification, a system that exists in all but the most primitive societies. Under social stratification, individuals or groups of individuals are ranked unequally according to wealth, education, and occupation and thus differ in status, power, and prestige.

Chapter 10 examines the concepts of social stratification and social class, and considers the opportunities an individual or group has to move from one social class to another. Chapter 11 is devoted to stratification based on racial or ethnic groups. An earlier chapter, Chapter 5, discusses stratification in terms of gender roles and stereotypes.

CHAPTER 10

Social Class and Social Mobility

Because social stratification is almost universal, sociologists have studied it extensively. This chapter presents the theories they have offered to explain it and the methods they have devised to study it in all its variations. The chapter then identifies the five social classes found in the United States and gives the lifestyle characteristics for each. Finally, it compares the costs and benefits of open and closed stratification systems and examines the critical factors in achieving upward mobility in a society.

Social Class

Social class refers to a segment of the population that differs from other segments of the same population in terms of shared values, prestige, associational activities, accumulated wealth and other personal possessions, and social etiquette. Different societies exhibit different social class arrangements.

In American society, the three basic indicators of social class are income, occupation, and education. Other significant variables include race, religion, nationality, sex, location of residence, and family background.

Social Stratification

In a social stratification system, individuals are ranked in accordance with the degree of desirable qualities that they possess and are placed in an appropriate social class. Desirable qualities are culturally determined. In the United States, desirable qualities include a good education, a high income, a large amount of wealth, and participation in a high-prestige occupation. In other cultures, however, desirable qualities may include the number of wives a man has or the number of cattle a family owns. Whatever the desirable qualities are defined as in a society, they are not shared equally by all members of a given society.

As noted in Chapter 4, *status* refers to the social position that an individual holds in a group, or the social ranking of a group when it is compared with other groups. A status is the position an individual occupies in the stratification system. Status indicates how the individual or group is ranked in relation to others with whom he/she is being compared. The status of an individual helps to determine a person's lifestyle, values, behavior patterns, privileges, and power.

Functional and Conflict Theories of Stratification

Two opposing theories have been offered to explain social stratification.

Functional Theory.   Sociologists who are functional theorists believe that social stratification exists in order to better satisfy the needs of society. They hold that rewards such as income, power, and status should be unequally distributed among the members of society in order to ensure that the most important positions are filled by the most qualified persons available. Social stratification, therefore, is functional to society.

Conflict Theory.   Conflict theorists believe that rewards should be equally distributed among the members of society. According to these theorists, inequality is not functional to society but is merely a matter of the wealthy and the powerful exploiting the poor and the weak.

Conflict theorists do not believe that the survival of society is contingent on the unequal distribution of rewards.

Karl Marx and Social Class

Karl Marx identified conflict between the classes as an inevitable condition. He believed that an individual's social class position was dependent on his/her relationship to the means of production. Thus, the owners of the natural resources and the factories would occupy the higher class positions. Marx divided society into essentially two classes, the owners of the means of production (the bourgeoisie) and the workers (the proletariat). He proposed that the bourgeoisie controlled the government, the church, the educational institutions, and the economy. Marx predicted, however, that the proletariat would become conscious of itself as a class being exploited by the bourgeoisie and would rise up in revolution, overthrow the bourgeoisie, establish a government of the proletariat, and start a classless society.

Max Weber and Social Class

While Marx defined a type of stratification that was based solely on economic criteria, Max Weber[1] identified three basic elements: wealth, power, and prestige. According to Weber, a person may rank high on one variable and low on another. Yet each element may influence the other two.

Methods of Studying Stratification

Three basic methods have been used by sociologists to study the class structure within a society: the reputational, the subjective, and the objective.

The Reputational Method. In this method, individuals are asked in which social class other people should be placed. When used in small communities, where most people know most other people, the reputational method is a useful tool. However, it is often not a workable method of studying social stratification in a large urban area, where people do not usually have personal knowledge of others living in the same community.

---

1   Max Weber, *Essays in Sociology* (1904), trans. and ed. by Talcott Parsons (New York: Charles Scribner's Sons, 1956).

Sociologists using the reputational method must be aware that those in the upper social classes are looking down at the bulk of the population, while those in the lower social classes are looking up. Thus, there is a tendency for those at either end of the continuum to have a biased view of the society. Sociologists have found, however, that there is a surprising consistency in the ranking of the vast majority of the population, even when this bias is present.

The Subjective Method. This is a self-classification approach. Individuals are asked to place themselves in the social class to which they think they belong. The wording of the response categories has turned out to be a critical factor in where people place themselves. When subjects are provided with only three response categories (lower class, middle class, and upper class), they tend to select middle class as their rank. Based on these responses, one would be led to believe that the United States is essentially a middle class society. However, when working class is added as a fourth response category, the results are very different; many individuals choose that category rather than middle class. The subjective method has proven to be especially useful when large, heterogeneous populations are sampled.

The Objective Method. In the objective method, the sociologist determines the criteria to be used for establishing class membership and the number of classes into which the population will be divided. Individuals are measured on a scale of established social class criteria, then placed in the appropriate social class according to their ranking on these criteria. This method was used by both W. Lloyd Warner[2] and August B. Hollingshead.[3] As is the case in all studies that use the objective method, the social class criteria used by the researcher will significantly influence the results. However, these criteria are selected after extensive research aimed at determining their appropriateness. As previously stated, the criteria typically used as social class criteria in American society are education, income, and occupation.

---

2   W. Lloyd Warner, Marcia Meeker, and Kenneth Eells, *Social Class in America* (Chicago: Science Research Associates, 1949).

3   August B. Hollingshead, *Elmstown's Youth* (New York: John Wiley & Sons, Inc., 1949).

Social Class in the United States

Researchers generally agree that the population of the United States can be divided into the upper class, upper-middle class, lower-middle class, working class, and lower class. The following gives typical characteristics of members of each social class in the United States. It must be recognized, however, that not all individuals in a particular social class hold the same values, attitudes, and beliefs. Moreover, a person who sees himself/herself as a member of one social class may be seen by others as belonging to a different social class.

The Upper Class

The upper class is characterized by its accumulation of wealth, influence in both the public and private sectors of society, small size, high income, high level of education, and stability of family life. Sociologists have divided this class into two groups, the upper-upper and the lower-upper classes.

The Upper-Upper Class.   The upper-upper class consists of families with very "old" names (they have a long history of wealth and influence). Members of the upper-upper class are born into it. The family names generally associated with the upper-upper class include the Rockefellers, Roosevelts, and Fords.

The Lower-Upper Class.   The lower-upper class consists of families with "new" names (they have acquired their wealth and influence more recently). Many members of the lower-upper class may actually have more highly valued material possessions and wealth than do members of the upper-upper class, but because they were not born into one of the "society" families, they do not generally attain upper-upper class membership until they intermarry with members of that class.

The Middle Class

Since the turn of the century, the growth of industry and big business in the United States has been accompanied by a corresponding need for administrative, managerial, and professional personnel. This need has let to an increase in the number of people who hold middle class membership. We tend to think of the United States as being a middle class society with associated middle class values and attitudes.

Belief in the value of hard work, education, family life, and honesty are characteristic of the middle class.

The Upper-Middle Class. The upper-middle class is characterized by high income, high level of education, low level of unemployment, and a high value placed on saving and planning for the future. Members of the upper-middle class are employed in professional or managerial positions, are politically active, and have a high level of participation in community activities.

The Lower-Middle Class. The lower-middle class consists primarily of white-collar and clerical workers, small businessmen and businesswomen, sales representatives, teachers, and middle-level management employees.

The values held by members of the upper-middle class are generally shared by those in the lower-middle class. Members of the lower-middle class value saving and planning for future needs, earn a moderate income, and attempt to secure additional education beyond high school.

The Working Class

The working class consists primarily of blue-collar and semiskilled workers who may be found in almost any business or industry. The vast amount of manual labor performed in the United States, from work in coal mines and on construction sites to work in factories and on farms, is carried out by the members of the working class. (Within this category are a limited number of highly skilled workers who usually receive a much higher rate of pay than other working class people.) Members of the working class earn a fairly low income, are unable to accumulate savings, attempt to satisfy their immediate needs rather than plan for the future, achieve a low level of education, and use credit extensively.

The Lower Class

The lower class is at the bottom of the social status ladder in the American stratification system. Members of the lower class earn either no income or so little income that they are considered to be at the poverty level. They tend to have no savings and have little education, and they are generally in poor health. The majority of the social welfare, equal-opportunity, and affirmative-action programs enacted by the

Congress of the United States and the legislatures of the individual states are directed at providing assistance to and raising the economic standards of the members of the lower class.

Social Class, Life Chances, and Lifestyles

The social class into which one is born has a profound influence on one's entire life. One faces more disadvantages and fewer life chances at the bottom of the social stratification system. One's mental health, education, occupation, political behavior, religious affiliations, social participation, and attitudes are all affected by one's social class. In general the higher an individual's social status, the longer is his/her life expectancy. Poor nutrition, inadequate housing, and insufficient medical treatment contribute to higher infant mortality rates in the lower classes.

Life chances refer to the various opportunities that a person has to move ahead in life and achieve his/her goals. Included are the chance to receive a college education, the chance to live a long and healthy life, the chance to enter a profession, and the chance to marry within or outside one's social class. The availability of these life chances is unevenly distributed, being highly dependent on one's social class.

Furthermore, each class is a unique subculture because it shares certain basic values and lifestyles. Lifestyle includes ways of spending leisure time, socialization practices, participation in clubs and political activities, and the manner of spending money, consuming goods, and practicing religion. Each social class has a unique way of engaging in these activities.

Social Mobility

The term "social mobility" refers to the movement of individuals from one social class to another. Individuals may move up or down, or remain at the same level but in a different occupation. Sociologists study how various structural and social factors contribute to the social mobility of groups or individuals. They also compare the rate of mobility in the United States with that in other countries.

Types of Social Mobility

Sociologists have identified several types of mobility: vertical, horizontal, intergenerational, and intragenerational.

Vertical Mobility

Vertical mobility refers to the change in status of an individual as he/she moves up or down the social ladder. For example, the manager of the meat department who is promoted to general manager of the supermarket has achieved upward vertical mobility. The promotion is accompanied by an increase in income and overall responsibility. On the other hand, the major league baseball player who is sent back to the minor leagues has suffered downward vertical mobility.

Horizontal Mobility

Horizontal mobility refers to social movement on the same social plane. An individual who makes an occupational change that doesn't affect his/her social status displays horizontal mobility. For example, a gas station attendant who becomes a construction worker at a higher hourly rate has displayed horizontal mobility.

Intergenerational Mobility

Intergenerational mobility refers to social mobility that takes place between generations. When the daughter of a taxicab driver earns a college education and goes on to become a successful medical doctor, intergenerational mobility has occurred. Downward intergenerational mobility may also take place, as in the case of a taxicab driver whose father is a physician.

Intragenerational Mobility

Intragenerational mobility refers to a change or changes in the social status of an individual or group of individuals within the same generation. For example, suppose that five children are born into one family of rather moderate means. After high school, four of the children enter the job market at medium-low levels, while the fifth child works part-time while attending college. After college graduation, the fifth child enters a major corporation at a rather high level, and after three years, he/she is promoted to a top managerial position. While he/she has attained upward vertical mobility, his/her brothers and sisters have remained at the same socioeconomic level.

Open and Closed Societies

All societies have some system of social stratification. They may be categorized as open or closed.

Open Societies

In an open society, certain inequalities may exist, but individuals have the opportunity to move up to a higher social class or down to a lower one. (A truly open society, however, is an ideal type, one that exists in theory only.) Within the open system, individuals can move from one class to another through hard work, demonstrated merit, luck, or marriage. Their status is thus said to be achieved. The United States has an open stratification system, not without barriers to be overcome.

Several disadvantages and liabilities accompany increased mobility.

1. Some individuals who compete for high social status simply do not possess sufficient ability and may experience a feeling of loss and frustration.

2. Those who can compete may feel they are giving up their principles, reducing the time spent with their families, or surrendering other values in order to devote more energy to achieving higher status.

3. Once a person reaches a goal, he/she may experience downward mobility.

4. Persons who move from a lower to a higher social class may change their interests and behavioral patterns, thereby losing some of their friends.

Closed Societies

In a closed society, a person's social status is assigned at birth and set for life with no possibility of moving either up or down. This condition is referred to as ascribed status (see Chapter 4).

A *caste* stratification system, where individuals cannot freely move from one level to another, is an example of a closed stratification system. A person born into a particular caste must remain in it for life. Intermarriage between members of castes is forbidden. The caste system of India, which was officially abolished by the government in 1949, was a basic part of life for over 2,500 years. Of the four main castes, the highest was the Brahmin (consisting of the scholars and the priests), and the lowest, the Harijan. The Harijans were the outcasts of society, and they are still often referred to as the untouchables. So low were they on the social ladder that even to be touched by their shadow required purification.

Factors Related to Social Mobility

Many social and structural factors determine just how much opportunity for mobility exists in a society for an individual or group of individuals. The most important factors appear to be societal industrialization, education, family background, and gender.

Industrialization

Sociologists have found that preindustrial or agricultural societies are most likely to have a closed stratification system. Typically, individuals in rural societies will occupy the same social status throughout their lives. Status is based on ascription, family background being the most significant factor to be considered. On the other hand, individuals who reside in urbanized, industrialized areas where status is most likely based on achievement usually have the opportunity to move from one social class to another.

As societies move toward urban industrialization, the proportion of people in the lower socioeconomic classes needed to perform unskilled labor is reduced. Employment in industrialized societies is largely based on possession of specialized skills that are acquired through education or training, and unskilled labor tasks are in many cases performed by machines and computers. Many individuals then have an opportunity to either move into a skilled occupation or enter the professional or managerial category.

Education

An individual's education is positively correlated with the income that he/she is likely to earn. Education increases social mobility by providing the individual with the skills necessary to enter the job market and to compete against others for a particular job. Most jobs require formal education provided by the school systems, although some jobs require experience that can only be acquired through work in the particular field. Occupational categories requiring a high level of education usually offer correspondingly higher salaries. Virtually all professions require a person to complete a given level of formal education prior to practicing that profession. In addition, the great majority of businesses require a person to complete a college education before entering the managerial level.

Family Background

Research on social mobility suggests that social class and the opportunity for mobility are to a large extent linked to inheritance. The occupations of an individual's father and mother influence the amount of education that person receives, which in turn affects his/her job opportunities. Furthermore, the size of an individual's family is an important social factor related to mobility. When there are many children in the same family, it is often difficult for parents to provide for all the needs of all of the children. If the children are close in age, it may be especially difficult for the family to provide them with the financial resources needed to acquire a good education and move on to a rewarding job. Thus, children who come from a small family (more often found in an urban area) are more likely to achieve vertical mobility than are children who come from a large family.

Race and ethnic family background are also critical factors that influence one's chances of achieving vertical mobility. In the United States, a long history of discrimination against minority groups such as Blacks, Native Americans, and Hispanics exists in business, industry, and schools. The chances of members of these groups securing a good education or job are not as great as they may be for white Americans. (Race and ethnicity will be discussed in Chapter 11).

Gender

Gender is also an important factor in social mobility. In American society, males and females receive different types of socialization regarding employment and family. Until very recently, males took for granted that they were to be the primary wage earner and were to assume overall responsibility for the family's financial stability. Females were traditionally not encouraged to pursue a higher education or enter a career. Recently, there has been an increase in dual career families (families where both wife and husband have careers) and females in higher social statuses. Despite this change, however, the opportunities that females receive for social mobility are still not equal to those of males.

A female's age at the time of marriage is also an important factor in determining the likelihood of social mobility. Research suggests that the younger the female is at the time of marriage, the lower the probability of her gaining upward mobility. Females and males may also achieve vertical mobility by marrying into a social class higher than their own.

Social Mobility in the United States

Most Americans believe that their chances for achieving upward social vertical mobility are great. As in most industrial societies, the possibility for social mobility certainly exists in the United States, but perhaps to a lesser extent than once thought. Although intergenerational mobility has been identified, the actual extent of this mobility has been rather moderate. Certain factors inhibit the mobility of certain groups and individuals. The government, however, has made available a wide variety of programs to help middle class and lower class people attain social mobility. Included in these programs are college-loan programs (although cut in recent years) and affirmative-action programs.

It must be recognized that social mobility may include movement in either an upward or a downward direction. In an open stratification system, as in the United States, there must be a certain level of downward mobility if the society is to maintain itself.

CHAPTER 11

Race and Ethnic Relations

Racial and ethnic group membership is a prominent factor in the stratification process of many societies. Prejudice, discrimination, stereotypes, ethnocentrism, and racism perpetuate these social differences. This chapter discusses the concepts of race and ethnicity, the consequences of ethnic diversity in societies, and the types of relationships that can occur between dominant and minority groups. In a given society, the dominant group can prevent minority groups from freely and equally participating in what that society has to offer, or it can include them. Minority groups can also react in a variety of ways to the dominance and discrimination directed at them. Their dilemma is often whether to remain a distinct cultural group or to assimilate into the mainstream culture.

Basic Concepts

Sociologists make use of the concepts of race, ethnic groups, minority groups, racism, ethnocentrism, stereotypes, prejudice, and discrimination.

Race

A race is a category of individuals who through generations of inbreeding, share certain common physical or biological characteristics. Racial groups are generally discussed in terms of three broad categories: the white or Caucasian race, the black or Negroid race, and the yellow and brown or Mongoloid race. However, the variation within these racial categories is great because of migration, interbreeding, and overlapping. Whereas the biologist or physical anthropologist uses physical characteristics to categorize individuals by race, the sociologist emphasizes socially defined and perceived differences. These socially defined categories rather than the physical characteristics with which they may be linked form racial distinctions among people.

Ethnic Groups

An ethnic group is a number of people who have developed their own subculture; it is distinguished by the cultural characteristics that its members share. These characteristics can include religion, customs, language, and national background.

Minority Groups

A minority group is a category of individuals that because of its members' cultural or physical characteristics is somehow distinguished from a population of which it is a part. A minority group is not necessarily a numerical minority. Instead, a minority group usually lacks power relative to the dominant group in a society, and it is often denied full and equal participation. A minority may experience economic, religious, or political discrimination. In reality, the United States is a society made up of dozens of different minority groups, some of which are distinguished by their race and ethnicity, others by their economic, political, or occupational background. Some racial and ethnic minority groups in the United States are Blacks, American Indians (now called Native Americans), Mexicans, Puerto Ricans, Poles, Irish, and Jews. Other minority groups, such as low-income Americans and poorly educated Americans, are not racially or ethnically defined but are set apart because of their shared characteristics or background.

Racism and Ethnocentrism

Racism is the belief that the racial group to which one belongs is superior to other racia. groups. This response is consistent with the ethnocentric tendencies of most groups, which assume that their customs, appearance, and way of life are superior to all others. Ethnocentrism often prevents both the dominant and the minority groups from making the important compromises necessary for successful interaction and exchange.

Racism has been justified by the dominant group on the grounds that the minority group members are mentally inferior and can neither care for themselves nor make significant contributions to a society. These justifications may arise, however, because the dominant group feels that the minority group poses a threat to their position of economic advantage and authority. Thus, because of this fear, the dominant group may assert that the minority group members should be placed under direct supervision and control.

Stereotypes

Stereotypes are generalizations made concerning individuals in certain religious, racial, or ethnic categories. Members of the category are expected to display certain preconceived personality characteristics or behavioral patterns. Common stereotypes that have emerged in American society at one time or another suggest that Blacks are lazy, athletic, and musically inclined; that Poles are stupid; and that the Scots are stingy. The truth of the matter is that most Blacks work very hard to support their families and many are not interested in either athletics or music; there are brilliant Polish students at our colleges and universities; and many individuals of Scottish descent are among the more charitable members of society.

Assumptions have been made concerning the relationship between intelligence and race or between personality and race. However, social science research has found no clear evidence of such a relationship.

Prejudice and Discrimination

Prejudice refers to an attitude or feeling that a person has toward members of a minority group. Prejudice means to prejudge, and in doing so, a person makes certain assumptions about a member of another group before he/she has had an opportunity to actually meet that person.

Whereas prejudice implies an attitude, discrimination refers to an overt behavioral pattern that is directed towards all members of a minority group. This behavioral pattern is usually characterized by unjust or unfavorable treatment to the members of the minority group. Discriminatory practices that are still found in the United States include restrictive membership policies in certain churches, schools, or clubs; limiting the type of person allowed in a restaurant or recreational facility; discriminating in employment practices; and denying access to a political office and the political process.

Patterns of Racial and Ethnic Group Relations

Intergroup relations can take many forms. The dominant group can prevail in two ways: (1) by preventing a minority group from participating freely and equally in society by eliminating that group and (2) by absorbing (assimilating) the minority group, provided the minority group shares enough cultural characteristics with the dominant group that its distinctiveness disappears.

The minority and dominant groups can coexist in a society without the minority groups' losing their distinct characteristics. Examples are pluralism, if the groups interact on an equal basis, and ethnic or racial stratification, if the groups interact on an unequal basis, as in segregation. All these processes will be discussed below.

Minority Group Elimination

A minority group can "disappear" by being forcibly excluded or by being assimilated.

Expulsion and Annihilation

To prevent certain minority groups from participating in a society, the dominant group may eliminate them by expulsion or annihilation.

Expulsion occurs when one ethnic group forcefully evicts the less powerful group from its homeland, so that the minority is forced to live in a less desirable geographic area. For example, during the settling of the American western frontier, entire Indian tribes were driven from their land and forced to live on what we now call reservations.

Annihilation is the deliberate murder of members of an ethnic group by the dominant group. When this process is aimed at an ethnic minority group, it is called *genocide*. During World War II, the Nazis embarked on a campaign to murder all Jews. This program of annihilation, called the "Final Solution" by the Nazis, resulted in the deaths of more than six million Jews. In another example of this extreme behavior, reports state that Idi Amin, the dictator of Uganda, instigated a program to annihilate all Indians living in his African nation.

Assimilation and Amalgamation

A minority group can be absorbed into the mainstream of society by assimilation and amalgamation.

Assimilation is the merging of two different cultures into a single culture containing characteristics of both. When a minority ethnic group is assimilated into the dominant culture, the minority group loses its distinctiveness. Through assimilation, cultures can blend and lose their separate identities. Assimilation can also sometimes be an exchange process, with minority groups eventually acquiring the customs of the majority group, and the majority group eventually acquiring some of the customs of the minority group. This exchange has occurred to a large extent in the United States. After arriving in this country, new ethnic groups have both adopted American customs and influenced Americans to adopt some of their customs. Irish, Italians, Poles, Germans, and Chinese, along with many others, have participated in this process.

Amalgamation refers to intermarriage between different racial groups. The result of this process is the appearance of individuals with unique physical characteristics—characteristics different from those of the original groups.

Minority Group Coexistence

Minority groups can also participate in society without losing their distinctiveness. The following practices represent various means of including the members of minority groups as participants in society.

Cultural Pluralism

Cultural pluralism refers to a form of accommodation in which different racial or ethnic groups live together, each maintaining its own customs, while at the same time accepting the others' way of life as suitable for the society in which they live. The groups retain their distinctiveness and coexist in society without discrimination. Switzerland is the country that most sociologists point to as the ideal example of cultural pluralism. In Switzerland, there is no one national language, and different religious groups have been able to live together in relative peace and harmony.

Integration

Integration is a social arrangement in which both minority and dominant groups live together in harmony and view themselves as one culture, each making contributions to the culture. In a truly integrated society, all groups have equal access to the political, religious, economic, and educational institutions. Minority groups most similar to the dominant group have been the ones most easily integrated into American society. This similarity may be in terms of religion, nationality, race, or some cultural trait. Integration is also more easily attained if the incoming group is relatively small, speaks the same language as the dominant group, and does not compete for scarce valuables or scarce resources.

Segregation

Different ethnic groups can also coexist unequally in a society. Segregation is the practice of forcing members of the less powerful group to establish separate residences and to use separate facilities, including schools, hospital wards, and hotels. In most instances, the residences and facilities set aside for the minority are inferior to the ones enjoyed by the dominant group. Even though legislation and Supreme Court decisions have placed "legal limits" on the practice of segregation in the United States, the fact is that to a certain extent it still does exist.

Minority Group Reactions

Minority groups may react in a variety of ways to the dominance and discrimination directed at them in society. Some of the most obvious types of reactions are acculturation, self-segregation, separatism, and the creation of organizations.

Acculturation

Through acculturation, the minority group displays an acceptance and adoption of the dominant culture and lifestyle. This process can be difficult and distressing: members of the minority group have to give up their traditional way of life and thereby lose much of the pride they once had in their culture. Also, those who begin to acculturate risk losing the love and support of family members and friends who do not wish to relinquish the old ways. These individuals often find themselves stranded between the world they are leaving and the world they are entering. In an attempt to be accepted by the dominant group, minority group members may change their name or alter their physical appearance. Some blacks, for example, will straighten their hair or lighten the tone of their skin, and Jews and Poles have been known to change their names.

Self-Segregation

Through self-segregation, the members of the minority group voluntarily separate themselves from the rest of society to establish their own facilities and maintain their existing customs. It is not always clear, however, whether a group has voluntarily separated from society or has tacitly been forced to be apart. For example, some Native Americans are said to have elected to remain on their reservations rather than enter the general society. By staying on the reservations, they can preserve and maintain their languages, customs, traditions, and beliefs. Nevertheless, if Native Americans are not treated equally in the general society, and society does not support their equal and independent participation, it is hard to determine whether this segregation is voluntary or not.

Separatism

Through separatism, a new society is established by a minority group, often by the creation of boundaries. The members feel a sense of belonging and share a set of common goals. Separatism may be attained through partitioning a country into two different paths—one part for the dominant group and one part for the minority group. It may also be attained if members of a minority group migrate to a new land together and start their own new society.

Canada is an ideal country in which to examine the question of separatism. The French Canadian population is concentrated in Quebec, while the British Canadian population is prevalent in most other provinces. In recent years, many French Canadians have spoken out in favor of seceding from Canada and establishing Quebec as an independent nation.

Creation of Organizations

The minority group can collectively attempt to bring about changes in a society through the creation of organizations dedicated to the minority's specific goals. These organizations will set forth their aims, line up public support for their cause, and work in favor of legislation that supports their views. Examples are the National Association for the Advancement of Colored People (NAACP), which has played a major role in lobbying for legislation that will support black people, and the Anti-Defamation League (ADL) of B'nai B'rith, which has attempted to protect Jews from discrimination and has supported their rights.

Changing Relations Between Racial and Ethnic Groups

Two types of change are responsible for altering the relationships between various racial and ethnic groups: enacted change and crescive change.

Enacted Change

Enacted change is intentionally planned to alter the relationships between different racial and ethnic groups. Legislation prohibiting certain kinds of discrimination against minority groups, or permitting bilingual education, affirmative action, and racial group busing are all examples of enacted changes that have occurred within the United States in recent years.

Crescive Change

Crescive change is unplanned and takes place through the natural course of events. An example of crescive change is the loss of some ethnic stereotypes as minority and dominant groups work, attend school, and live together. These types of natural change do not occur often because specific actions are usually required or stereotypes become confirmed by selective perception.

Part V:
Change

The previous section discussed the important concepts of culture and social structure as key elements in any society. This section focuses on change in society, specifically social and cultural change. Chapter 12 presents the general processes of social and cultural change and their consequences for society. Chapter 13 looks at population change, change within natural environments, and changing communities. Chapter 14 explores change due to various degrees of organized behavior.

CHAPTER 12

Social and Cultural Change

Sociologists are concerned with change that occurs in both the structure and the culture of a society. The distinction between social and cultural change is not a sharp one, however, because most changes are the result of both cultural and structural forces. A more important distinction is that between change and progress. The word "progress" is a value judgment rather than a statement of fact, and it assumes that a society and its members are enriched, advanced, or improved by a change. "Change," on the other hand, is a nonevaluative term that signifies a modification or transformation of an existing culture or structure. This chapter discusses theories that have developed to interpret change, the agents of change, the factors that influence the rate of change within societies, and the reasons for resistance to change.

Definitions

Social change refers to a change in the social structure or social organization of a society. It is concerned with change as it affects a significantly large number of individuals in a given society. Changes that affect only a small number of people are not normally investigated by sociologists. Examples of social change include changes in the number of young people entering college, changes in the death rate of a population or the life expectancy of a population, and changes in the role of the female in the modern American family.

Cultural change refers to change in the culture of a society. Examples of cultural change are the invention of television, the introduction of new words or art forms, and the emergence of new norms regarding roles in society.

Although these definitions of social and cultural change are useful, when we look at actual changes in society, it is difficult to distinguish between those that are purely social in nature and those that are purely cultural. The concepts are interrelated, and change within society is often the result of both. The changing role of the female in the modern American family, for example, is a result of both structural changes (change in the organization of the social institution of the family) and cultural changes (change in the cultural norms regarding the roles of males and females). Consequently, sociologists often use the term sociocultural change to refer to change that has both social and cultural roots.

Theories of Social Change

Sociologists have developed a number of theories to explain why social change occurs and to help them predict what types of social changes may take place in the future. The four major approaches are referred to as evolutionary theories, cyclical theories, equilibrium theories, and conflict theories.

Evolutionary Theories

Auguste Comte, Herbert Spencer, and Karl Marx developed evolutionary theories to explain the process of social change in society. These theories envisioned society as developing through stages, from the simple to the more complex, becoming more and more progressive. The implication was that the higher the stage of development, the more superior the society.

Auguste Comte

The evolutionary theory of Auguste Comte saw society as passing through three successive stages: a theological, a metaphysical, and a scientific stage. In the theological stage, humans looked to God or to the supernatural, religion being the source of all knowledge concerning society and human existence. In the metaphysical stage, reasoning or logic was the basis by which all knowledge concerning society was gathered and interpreted. In the scientific stage (which was believed to be the most progressive stage), all knowledge was based on scientific or observable evidence rather than on religion or logic.

Hebert Spencer

Hebert Spencer applied Darwin's theories of organic evolution to the social evolution of societies. Societies moved from simple to the more complex by the elimination of those individuals who were lazy and unfit and the rewarding of those who were productive.

Karl Marx

Although Marx is classified as a conflict theorist, he developed an evolutionary theory of social change. Based on successive changes in technology, societies progressed from the simple to the more complex. At each stage, a society contained the conditions to destroy itself; eventually, these conditions produced change and led a society into the next stage. Although Marx viewed capitalism as exploitative, he saw it as a necessary stage for the eventual progression to communism. Inevitably, he held, capitalism will be overthrown, resulting in communism.

Each of the evolutionary theories pictures a very simplified pattern of societal development, one that does not reflect the actual complexity involved in that development. Moreover, evolutionary theories tend to be ethnocentric in portraying modern societies as superior to those of the past. Though present society is different, it is not necessarily better.

Cyclical Theories

Evolutionary theories view societies as progressing along a linear course, moving forward, not backward. The cyclical theories also view society as passing through different stages, but the stages are seen as part of repetitive cycles. According to cyclical theorists such as Spengler and Toynbee, society does not stop developing once it reaches a final stage; rather, it cycles back to the beginning stage.

Although these cyclical theories are interesting, they leave many questions unanswered, and evidence to support them is unreliable. For example, although these theories explain the process of change, they fail to explain why these repetitive cycles occur.

Functional Theories

Functional theories view society as being in a state of constant equilibrium. Society is made up of a number of interdependent parts, each of which contributes to the effectiveness of the whole. If social change disrupts one of the parts, the society is thrown into imbalance, and additional social changes take place in other parts to compensate. Social change only temporarily disrupts the harmonious arrangement of interdependent parts, and succeeding social changes help society to move again to a state of harmony and equilibrium.

Conflict Theories

Conflict theories do not see society as a harmonious arrangement of groups and processes. Instead, they view society as a conglomeration of groups that are continuously in conflict. Social change occurs as these groups compete with one another for scarce goods and resources (such as power and money). Society is relatively unstable and disorganized because groups are continually attempting to change the status quo.

Agents of Change

Change may be introduced into a society by diffusion, invention, or discovery.

Diffusion

Diffusion is the introduction and spread of a trait from an external culture. Cultures are constantly coming in contact with one another, either within one society or between societies, and the transmission of cultural traits is very common. Specific types of clothing that you wear, such as moccasins (Indian); the music that you listen to, such as salsa (Latin-American); and the food that you eat, such as sushi (Japanese) are all cultural traits diffused from other cultures. Americans have borrowed much of their existing culture from other societies.

Invention

An invention is the creation of something new by combining two or more elements that already exist within a culture. Elements that already exist are constantly being combined in different ways to produce new objects or new ways of doing things that have applications for society and may produce change within society. Thus, inventions may be material, such as the telephone and the computer, or social, such as the constitutional form of government and the use of mediators for divorce settlements.

Discovery

A discovery is knowledge that already exists in a culture but is finally verified and put to use. A discovery adds something new to a culture. Although the information existed, it was never implemented. For example, a discovery often refers to physical matters—the discovery of fire, electricity, and the law of gravity.

Factors in the Rate of Social and Cultural Change

A basic task of the sociologist is to identify the primary causal factors in social and cultural change. Social change is such a complex process, however, that no single factor can explain it in its entirety. The following are some of the more pertinent causal factors.

Physical Environment

The physical environment subjects a population to a set of conditions that will be either more or less conducive to change. Extremes of temperature, storms, and earthquakes all influence humans to change their lifestyles or behavior patterns. Furthermore, the distribution and availability of the natural resources determine to a large degree the type of life people lead and how societies evolve and change.

Technology

Many technological innovations have helped to produce widespread social and cultural change. For example, over the last twenty-five years, the use of television has significantly altered the nature of social relationships in the family and has become a major factor in socialization. Industrialization and technological advances in agriculture, manufacturing, transportation, and communications have all contributed to the trend toward urbanization. For instance, the automobile, an innovation in transportation, led to the growth of suburbs, increased geographic mobility, changed courtship patterns, created many new factory jobs and added to air pollution.

Ideology

A basic ideology, which is a complex set of beliefs and values, is present in every society. Ideologies may help maintain the status quo, or they may stimulate change if the beliefs and values are no longer compatible with the needs of the society. For example, communism and socialism were introduced and took root in many nations of the world only when the existing political ideologies no longer met people's needs.

Leadership

Dynamic and influential leaders can also serve as the impetus for social change. These leaders attract large followings who join with them in social movements (discussed in Chapter 14). Leaders such as Mao Tse-tung, Gandhi, Martin Luther King, Jr., and Thomas Jefferson inspired others to organize and take part in social movements.

Population

A dramatic, rapid, and large-scale change in population is itself a change in the organization or structure of a society (social change). Such radical change in population size can cause further social and cultural change. A rapid increase may necessitate new production techniques, whereas a rapidly declining population may call for significant changes in social organization so a society can defend itself from its enemies. In India, for example, the population was growing so rapidly that neither the distribution of its land nor its food production could keep pace. As a result of this crisis, innovations in both birth control techniques and food technology were introduced.

Cohort Changes

When sociologists measure change within culture, they must pay careful attention to cohort changes. A cohort is a group of people from the same subculture who were socialized at the same period of time. A cohort experiences the same social events and cultural values while growing up. Sociologists suggest that individuals within a cohort are more similar in their attitudes and behaviors than individuals between cohorts because of the experiences they share. For example, individuals (in one subculture) growing up during the Depression are likely to have similar attitudes regarding work and money—attitudes very different from those of individuals from the same subculture being socialized at present. As new cohorts are introduced into the culture (with new experiences and new attitudes), and as other cohorts withdraw, cultural change may occur.

Resistance to Change

Change is an inevitable part of all societies. The previous section examined a number of factors that influence the rate of social and cultural change within a society. Another consideration is the willingness of people to change. An innovation in a society can be accepted immediately or slowly, can be accepted in part, or can be rejected completely. The introduction of an innovation, therefore, does not necessarily lead to cultural or social change. (Behavior tied to a group of individuals who have gathered together to promote or prevent change will be discussed in Chapter 14.)

Societies may be resistant to social and cultural change for a number of reasons.

1. A society may lack the necessary human and physical resources necessary to maintain certain types of changes. For example, government officials may choose not to have a large factory built because of the lack of both the manpower to erect it and the physical resources to maintain it.

2. There may be a conflict between the values of a society and a proposed change. For example, the legalization of birth control may meet resistance when these policies are in direct conflict with moral values favoring large families and children.

3. Those who hold the economic and political power within a society may fear that change will in some measure reduce their power. Affirmative-action policies in the United States have met with much resistance because, in part, white males feel that these policies threaten their positions of economic advantage and political authority.

4. A society may want to preserve its culture and way of life by avoiding contact with innovations and inventions. If a society is isolated from other groups of people, new cultural elements will not be introduced. In the United States, the Amish keep themselves relatively isolated from the rest of society so that they will not be exposed to cultural traits in conflict with their own values. Some primitive societies still exist in mountainous or jungle areas where they are too isolated to be influenced by modernizing ways. These cultures may also be resisting cultural exchanges, because their present cultural system still satisfies their present needs.

Social Planning

Social planning is an attempt by social scientists to guide and direct the process of social change so that these changes will be advantageous to society. Social change is examined with an eye toward making the proposed change compatible with the existing values, goals, and objectives of a society. Even though the motives and objectives of social planners may be honest and true, the results of their projects are not always desirable. This is so because it is not possible to predict all of the consequences of a planned change.

What role should sociologists take in social planning? Some believe that they should advise both government and business officials concerning the desirability of implementing certain programs directed at social change. Others see their role not as giving advice and direction, but as providing results from their research that may predict the effects of certain programs.

CHAPTER 13

Population, Ecology, and Urbanization

In the last hundred years, change has been far-reaching in three areas that affect human society—in the population, in the natural environment, and in the structure of communities. These three areas of concern are known as demography, the study of the size, composition, and distribution of a given population; ecology, the study of the relationship between humans and their physical environment; and urban sociology, the study of city life.

The first section of this chapter discusses how demographic change occurs within a given population and the consequences of this change for society and the individual. The second section focuses on the interdependency between the population and the natural environment. The last section examines the process of urbanization, which occurs when large numbers of people leave the agricultural regions of a country to live in urban areas.

Demography

Demography, a specialized field within sociology, is the systematic study of populations. The demographer is concerned with the size, composition, and distribution of a given population, and with the social factors that influence these variables. Consequently, the sociologist who specializes in this important field studies both the effect of population changes on society and the effect of society on population. Perhaps the best example of a demographic study in the United States is the national census. Every ten years, the population of the United States is not only counted but divided into several categories, thus making it possible to characterize the population in terms of size, composition, and distribution.

National census data and the collection of annual vital statistics, such as the number of births and deaths, all contribute to the pool of available demographic data. Data of this nature are most useful when planning what goods and services (e.g., educational and medical services) a given population will require in future years. By gathering and studying statistics and current trends, the demographer can aid both government and private industry in their planning.

Demographic Variables

Demographers may focus on several biological and social variables in their studies of populations. Among the more important of these variables are sex distribution, age distribution, marital status, racial distribution, income group, occupation, size of household, and place of residence. These data give the demographer an accurate quantitative picture of the population under study.

Basic Demographic Concepts

The following are basic concepts used by demographers to refer to change in the population.

1. *Crude birthrate:* The number of live births per year, per 1,000 people in the population.

2. *Crude death rate:* The number of deaths per year, per 1,000 people in the population.

3. *Age-specific rate:* The birthrate or death rate for specific age

levels in the population. For example, the crude birthrate can be refined and be made age-specific and sex-specific by considering in a separate category only the women of childbearing age within a population.

4. *Standardized birthrates and death rates:* Adjusted rates that take into account the vital differences between populations that may affect their birthrates or death rates. For example, in a community made up primarily of young couples, the birthrate might appear to be high when compared to that of other populations. However, by calculating the standardized birthrate (comparing the same young age group in other populations), a more realistic picture of childbearing capacity will be developed.

5. *Life expectancy:* The number of years of life that the average infant born into a society may be expected to live.

6. *Life span:* The length of life that is possible for a given species.

7. *Sex ratio:* The number of males per each 100 females in a given population.

8. *Fertility:* The rate of reproduction in a society, that is, the number of actual births per 1,000 females of childbearing age.

9. *Fecundity:* The biological potential of women to reproduce. Although some women are capable of bearing more than twenty children during their childbearing years, the number of children actually born to an individual in most societies is far below this level.

10. *Optimum population:* The ideal population size for a given geographical area.

Measurement of Population Growth

There are three variables in the measurement of population growth or decline: births, deaths, and migration. If the crude birthrate plus the immigration rate is greater than the crude death rate plus the rate of out migration (emigration), a population is increasing. For example, while the western American states were being settled, there was tremendous population growth. Large numbers of families were migrating west, and having many children was an economic asset to these settlers. Even though the death rate was relatively high, the volume of immigration and the large families that grew in the newly settled territories maintained the high rate of population increase.

Migration

Migration is defined as the movement of people from one geographic location to another. Individuals offer many reasons for migrating, ranging from inadequate food to religious persecution. Basically, people migrate to find greater opportunities to live a better and more productive life.

Internal Migration

Internal migration is the movement from one region of a country to another, such as from New York State to North Carolina. Statistics indicate that in an average year, 20 percent of American families move. During the past six decades, families have tended to move from the agricultural regions of the South and Midwest to the urban-industrial cities of the Northeast and Far West. Recent trends suggest, however, that migration to the South (Sunbelt) and Southwest is on the rise. There has also been a rather large migration of Puerto Ricans from their native Caribbean island to the northeastern states on the American mainland, and in particular to New York City.

International Migration

International migration is the movement from one country to another. Both internal migration and international migration in large numbers will produce changes in population composition and may lead to additional social and economic problems. For example, the population shift may result in an excess of workers in the labor market, and individuals may have difficulty adjusting to local customs and a new and different way of life.

Technology and Population Growth

A significant factor in worldwide population growth is the advance in human technology. Technological developments have made food more abundant, raised the level of medical care, and generally heightened standards of living.

Improvements in medical technology have helped increase life expectancy, significantly reducing the proportion of deaths at birth or during early infancy, and curing many adult diseases. For example, just a few decades ago, diseases such as polio, diabetes, pneumonia, heart disease, and streptococcus infection meant almost certain death.

Not all the effects of these technological developments have been beneficial; these advances have also brought about air pollution, the disposal of toxic waste products in lakes and rivers, and disasters such as Three Mile Island.

Malthusian Theory

Rapid population growth may produce a number of rather serious social and ecological problems. Among these are high rates of unemployment, a depletion of the food supply and of other vital natural resources, inadequate housing, and stress and conflict that in turn may lead to serious emotional difficulties. In 1798, the Englishman Thomas Malthus published a book entitled *Essay on the Principles of Population*. In this work, Malthus stated that population would increase geometrically while the food supply would increase only arithmetically. The result would be a shortage of food. Malthus predicted that population and food supply would be brought back into balance as a result of war, pestilence, and famine. The predictions made by Malthus did not come true in countries such as the United States, because of innovations in agricultural technology and the widespread use of improved contraceptives. Changing attitudes toward birth control and the importance many women attach to pursuing a career have been factors in restricting population growth.

The Demographic Transition Theory

The movement from a rural to an urban society has also helped to slow population growth. In urban industrial societies, large numbers of children in a family are an economic liability rather than an economic asset. The demographic transition theory maintains that once a population becomes urban and industrial in character, the growth rate of that population will stabilize because parents will have only as many children as they believe they can support. This demographic transition process occurs in three different stages.

In stage one, there are both high birthrates and high death rates. The population is relatively stable. This stage is typical of the under-developed areas of the world.

In stage two, there are both high birthrates and low death rates. The death rates are low during this stage because of the introduction of life-saving technological innovations, and population will grow rather quickly.

In stage three, the rate of population growth levels off, with both lower birthrates and lower death rates. This stage occurs when societies become highly industrialized and large families are seen as an economic liability.

Population Policies

The number of children a family desires is the personal decision of parents. In most societies, however, governmental policies attempt to influence these decisions. Such policies can be either pronatal (in favor of increasing the birthrate) or antinatal (in favor of decreasing it).

Pronatal Policies

Pronatal policies are adopted by societies that perceive their birthrates to be too low. These pronatal policies may provide economic incentives to families who have (many) children, or they may restrict access to abortion and contraceptive clinics.

Antinatal Policies

Antinatal policies are adopted by societies that perceive their birthrates to be too high. To reduce birthrates, governments either (1) provide incentives to people who voluntarily accept sterilization, use contraceptive devices, or participate in family planning clinics; or (2) use coercion. If coercion is used, parents lose their right to determine how many children they will have. In the most basic form of coercion, the state might declare a quota on the number of children that may be born into each family and issue a license for each new child. Those families who have children past the designated quota might be subjected to forced sterilization or imprisonment. In most underdeveloped countries, forced family planning has proven unsuccessful.

Ecology

Ecology, like demography a specialized field within sociology, studies the relationship between all forms of life and the physical environment. The ecologist is concerned with how humans influence the physical environment, and in turn how the physical environment influences humans. Although ecology had its roots in the natural sciences, social scientists have been applying its principles to their study of human populations over the past century. The concept of environment, to a sociologist who studies ecology, extends past the social environment to include the physical environment as well.

The Ecosystem

The physical and social environment is a complex system of interrelationships called the ecosystem. The ecosystem is made up of all life forms that inhabit the environment. Animal and plant life, as well as water, air, and land, are part of the ecosystem. An ecosystem may be any size. A single drop of water from a brook and the island of Manhattan are both ecosystems, for the basic principle of mutual interdependence exists in each case.

Ecologists investigate social and environmental problems in terms of how change influences an entire ecosystem. Change can occur within the physical environment and affect the population, and vice versa, change can occur within the population and subsequently affect the physical environment. The science of ecology deals with major environmental and social problems that can result from change, such as pollution, overcrowding, depletion of natural resources, destruction of animal life, and destruction of land. For example, rapidly expanding populations tend to deplete quickly the available natural resources and create waste products that the physical environment cannot properly synthesize. Ecologists try to solve these problems by making people aware of the resources that must be preserved and by consulting on social legislation affecting these vital areas.

Urbanization

Urbanization is the process by which numbers of people leave the rural regions of the country to establish urban communities. The consequences of urbanization are a major concern of sociologists.

Rural and Urban Communities

A community may be defined as a specific group of people who reside in a given geographical area, share a common culture and way of life, are cognizant of the fact that they share a certain unity, and can act collectively in their pursuit of a goal. Examples of communities are towns, villages, cities, neighborhoods, and metropolitan regions.

Rural Communities

A rural community is most often characterized by involvement in agricultural pursuits, close family ties, and common values and traditions. It is a fairly homogeneous group of people with strong and harmonious interpersonal relationships. Although these qualities seem ideal, there were drawbacks to early rural society: isolation, little opportunity for privacy, and a lack of goods, services, and educational opportunities.

Urban Communities

The urban community is made up of a large heterogeneous population. Relationships among people tend to be impersonal, anonymous, and temporary. The great size of the urban population and the relative anonymity that it offers its members mean that the opportunity for committing criminal acts is much greater in cities than in rural areas. Statistics gathered by criminal justice agencies indicate that the incidence of crime in the major-offense categories is approximately four times greater in cities than in rural communities. Because of overcrowding, social disorganization, and high rates of unemployment, deviant behavior has flourished in large cities.

Factors Contributing to Urbanization

Urbanization has advanced worldwide in the last century or so. In the United States, a steady increase in the percentage of urban residents has been noted in each census since the early 1800s. In 1860, approximately 20 percent of the American population was urban; in 1900, about 40 percent. In 1920, more than half of the American people lived in cities, and by 1950, nearly 60 percent. These figures clearly demonstrate that year by year the American population is becoming more and more urbanized.

This urbanization has occurred partly because of population growth, but also because of the large number of technological innovations over the past century. The industrial revolution led to the rapid increase in urbanization. As factories and plants were built, large numbers of people relocated from the rural areas to work in these plants. Furthermore, technological advances in agriculture, manufacturing, transportation, and communication all contributed to the trend toward urbanization.

Disadvantages of Urban Life

Sociologists such as Durkheim, Redfield, Wirth, and Tonnies extensively studied the rural-urban transition in the early part of the twentieth century. They firmly believed that the transition had many undesirable consequences. They saw personal relationships being replaced by impersonal ones, and a previously orderly society turning chaotic.

When excessively large numbers of people crowd together in urban areas, life may be stressful. Urban life becomes anonymous and impersonal because individuals can only become acquainted with a small proportion of the people around them. This may lead to feelings of mutual distrust and result in total dissatisfaction with the quality of urban life. In addition, urban life is characterized by a high level of competition and conflict. This is primarily true because status is determined by one's achievements rather than being ascribed at birth, as is the case in many rural societies.

Advantages of Urban Life

There are many advantages to residing in an urban community. Among these are privacy, mobility, a wide range of lifestyles and careers, opportunities for creativity, cultural institutions (theaters, opera, ballet, etc.), excellent educational opportunities, specialized medical care, and superior recreational facilities.

Patterns of Urban Growth

Three basic theories attempt to describe the actual manner in which cities have grown: the concentric zone theory, the sector theory, and the multiple nuclei theory. It should be noted that these theories are applicable to some but certainly not all cities.

Concentric Zone Theory

The concentric zone theory was developed by Ernest Burgess[1] in 1925. Burgess viewed the city as consisting of a series of circular zones, each devoted to a specific use and each inhabited by a different segment of the population. Zone 1, the center zone, is the central business district. As the city grows, more zones are formed and spread outward from the central zone. Zone 2, referred to as a zone of transition, consists of deteriorating buildings and a high degree of social disorganization. Zone 3 is a residential zone consisting of the homes of working people. Zone 4, also a residential zone, is inhabited by members of the middle class. Zone 5 is essentially upper-class suburbs.

Many American cities have a central business area surrounded by a transition zone, which is in turn surrounded by several zones representing residential areas, each residential area consisting of a different social class and a different type of housing. The housing quality generally tends to improve as one moves outward from the central business district and slum area, but there are many exceptions to this pattern.

Sector Theory

The sector theory, developed by Homer Hoyt,[2] sets forth another pattern for city growth. Hoyt hypothesizes that cities will grow along their transportation routes rather than in circular zones. They will grow

---

1   Robert E. Park, Ernest W. Burgess, and R. D. McKenzie, *The City* (Chicago: The University of Chicago Press, 1925).
2   Homer Hoyt, *One Hundred Years of Land Values in Chicago* (Chicago: The University of Chicago Press, 1933).

outward in wedge-shaped sectors, each devoted to residential, commercial, recreational, or industrial purposes.

Multiple Nuclei Theory

The multiple nuclei theory was developed by Chauncey D. Harris and Edward L. Ullman.[3] They propose that there is no specific pattern to the growth of cities. Instead, cities have a number of specialized areas, each representing a nucleus. The specialized areas may be devoted to government, business, or industry. Whatever its specialization, each nucleus will influence the growth and development of its surrounding area.

Convergence of Rural and Urban Communities

Many of the characteristics, material goods, and lifestyles of urban centers are now beginning to appear in rural communities. This is occurring primarily because residents of rural communities now have easy access to cities through improved transportation and mass communication. As this process continues, there will be fewer and fewer distinctions between residents of the two areas.

3   Chauncey D. Harris and Edward L. Ullman, *The Nature of Cities,* Annals of the American Academy of Political and Social Science, 242: 7-17, November 1945.

CHAPTER 14

Collective Behavior and Social Movements

The previous two chapters discussed change as a continuous process within all societies. This chapter deals specifically with change that occurs through the behavior of many people. Collective behavior is characterized by unstructured, unpredictable, spontaneous, and emotional patterns of behavior. When engaged in collective behavior, individuals respond to a particular stimulus, person, or event that represents an issue with which they are commonly concerned. They engage in actions they would not normally perform when alone or in the course of daily life, where accepted norms, roles, and social control govern behavior. The relatively unstructured and unorganized character of collective behavior distinguishes it from institutional behavior.

Collective behavior itself can either be expressive in nature or aimed at producing or preventing social change. Both types of collective behavior are discussed in this chapter. The first section examines the nature of collective behavior, theories developed to explain it, and the behavior of individuals in crowds and masses. The second section discusses social movements: the different types, the stages of develop-

*ment through which they pass, and their consequences for both in-
dividuals and society at large.*

Collective Behavior

Collective behavior is the unstructured, spontaneous, emotional,
and unpredictable behavior of an aggregate of people in response to a
common stimulus, which can be a person, an action, or an event. It is
likely to take place when formalized, traditional means of doing things
are no longer adequate, and when individuals are emotionally
predisposed in some way, e.g., afraid, angry, happy, anxious. Examples
of collective behavior are mobs, riots, crazes, fads, fashions, mass
hysteria, and the development of public opinion.

The aggregate of individuals that engages in collective behavior is
referred to as the *collectivity*. The collectivity is a temporary, unstructured collection of individuals with no formal role division or hierarchy
of authority. Once the issue that brought them together has been settled,
the people in a collectivity disperse.

The results of collective behavior will be disadvantageous if
property is damaged or if individuals are hurt. However, collective
behavior is advantageous if it brings about needed changes in society.
For example, many collectivities protest because they feel they have
been treated unfairly. Protest can help to bring about needed changes in
legislation that will ensure that the collectivity will be treated more
fairly in the future.

Determinants of Collective Behavior

The sociologist Neil Smelser[1] cites six conditions as the primary
determinants of collective behavior: structural conduciveness, structural strains, generalized belief, precipitating factors, mobilization for
action, and operation of social control. These factors are described
below.

---

1   Neil J. Smelser, *Theory of Collective Behavior* (Free Press, New York,
1962).

Structural Conduciveness

The structure of the society must be such that a particular form of collective behavior may take place. For example, in the mid-1970s there was near panic in the United States because of the energy emergency and the gasoline shortage. The government hadn't enforced minimum miles-per-gallon requirements on the automobile manufactures, and therefore, most cars in service used a good deal of gasoline, which was no longer abundant. Long lines at the pumps and curtailed driving led to deep concern, augmented by the fact that gasoline had only been rationed during wartime; peacetime shortages were unheard of.

Structural Strains

When a strain is placed on society, people are often encouraged to work together to find an acceptable solution. Both the civil rights movement and the destruction of urban black ghettos in the 1960s are examples of people acting collectively because they were denied social and economic equality.

Generalized Belief

Before a solution to a problem can be found, there must be a general consensus that a problem does indeed exist. Thus, the problem must be identified, opinions formed, and possible solutions explored. For example, the pro-choice movement in the United States attracted a considerable following of both men and women who believed that it was essentially the woman's choice whether or not she would have a child. A generalized belief that supported this claim of free choice emerged, and various groups and individuals who supported it began to work against the laws that forbade abortions. The same process is true presently with a generalized belief supporting the claim that the unborn fetus is living and should therefore be allowed to be born.

Precipitating Factors

In order for collective behavior to emerge, some significant event must first drive individuals to respond collectively. A precipitating factor is the particular incident that incites individuals to express their pent-up feelings. Precipitating factors may suggest that something they value highly is being threatened. In this case individuals may act collectively to either preserve or gain back that which they value. Very often, this single event is exaggerated by rumor, which in turn makes the event even more dramatic. For example, when police officers are attempting to make an arrest in a racially tense neighborhood, a single encounter between a resident and the police is often enough to incite a riot involving many people. Most often the people rioting do not even see the encounter but instead have the details related to them by others.

Mobilization for Action

After the precipitating event has occurred, the group organizes for action. This type of hastily assembled organization is usually unstructured and fairly loose. In the above example with the police officers, the crowd is mobilized for action when leaders emerge and begin to direct its activities. Slogans will be shouted and voices raised in support of the minority group and against the police.

Operation of Social Control

Whether or not the collective efforts of individuals will be successful is largely dependent on the success or failure of the social control mechanisms within a society. These mechanisms of social control, including the police, government, and media, will together influence the outcome of the collective behavior. If a society's social control mechanisms (such as police) are strong enough, a riot will be suppressed. However, if enough riots break out in enough cities, the collective message will be so strong that government officials will be forced to take a serious look at the issues being raised by the rioters.

Theories of Collective Behavior

There are three theoretical perspectives that have been formulated by sociologists to explain collective behavior: the contagion theory, the convergence theory, and the emergent norm theory. No one theoretical perspective appears to effectively explain all collective behavior. However, by combining the factors relevant to each perspective, a comprehensive understanding of collective behavior is obtained.

Contagion Theory

Emotional contagion is the spread of emotional reactions from one person to another. The reactions of one person reinforce the reactions of the next, until all members of the collectivity are affected. Even when this occurs, reactions can still be heightened as individuals continue to reinforce one another. For example, as fear and anger are passed from person to person, more fear and anger are generated. Contagion theorists believe that collective behavior would be impossible if individuals did not stimulate and respond to one another and thus heighten each other's emotional intensity.

With stimulation, feelings become so intense that individuals no longer rationally consider what they are doing, and engage in behavior they would never engage in under ordinary circumstances. When individuals are in a crowd, the self-identity and self-control of each member may be lost. The following are characteristics typically found among the members of the crowd that may lead to this loss of self-identity and self-control.

Anonymity. Within crowds that are highly anonymous, there is a significant potential for nonconventional behavior. An individual acting within such a crowd stands a good chance of losing his/her sense of individual responsibility. The members of the Nazi regime, when later confronted with the seriousness of their crimes, typically placed all blame and responsibility on the crowd. Frequently, they hid behind an anonymous veil, claiming that they were pulled along by others through no fault of their own.

Impersonality. Membership and behavior in a collectivity are generally viewed as impersonal. The actions that the collectivity takes are not necessarily aimed at attacking or supporting a specific individual. The impersonal nature of collective action is exemplified during race riots, where chance is frequently the only criterion used by the hostile mob for singling out a particular member of a minority group to harass or attack.

Suggestibility. People in collectivities are likely to act upon suggestion because of the lack of well-established leadership, acceptable behavioral patterns, and individual responsibility. Furthermore, the suggestion is especially strong if it is made with a good deal of authority. During some riots, stores are looted and homes are burned at the suggestion of people who temporarily but forcefully assert their leadership. Members of the crowd do not stop to think about the consequences of their behavior; if the stores are forced to close, they will have no easy access to food, and if their homes burn, their families will be out on the street. Under more normal circumstances, the members of the crowd would not follow the suggestions or orders of such leaders.

Convergence Theory

Whereas the contagion theory focuses on how being in a crowd can drive individuals to act collectively, the convergence theory concentrates on how the similarity of individuals gathered together in a crowd leads to collective behavior. To convergence theorists, the major factor in explaining collective behavior is the grouping of similar people. Only those individuals prone to engaging in collective behavior and those individuals who hold certain attitudes will converge and behave collectively. Therefore, collective behavior results when a group of people gather together who have the same personality characteristics, attitudes, needs, and desires. For example, individuals attending a rock concert share common characteristics and desires. Thus, the convergence of like-minded people at these events facilitates collective behavior.

Emergent Norm Theory

Contagion theory and convergence theory both focus on the psychology of the individual in understanding collective behavior. The emergent norm theory, on the other hand, focuses on the norms for behavior that arise within a collectivity, and therefore, it is more sociological than psychological in nature. In situations where collective behavior can occur, group norms emerge regarding appropriate behavior. Emergent norm theorists propose that individuals act collectively because of the social pressure in a collectivity of individuals to comply with group norms. Individuals are hesitant to oppose emergent norms within a group. For example, when people wait in line for a clothing store to open its doors for a "final sale," they begin to look around to see what others are doing. Because of the anxiety and tension in this situation, instead of quietly moving into the store and shopping, a group norm emerges that allows individuals to push their way into the store and throw clothes every which way in order to find the best deals.

Crowd Behavior

A crowd is a gathering of individuals in close physical proximity who are for a limited period concerned with a particular event, person, or idea. The crowd reacts to events in an unstructured manner, and its members influence one another in their actions. Crowds include large aggregates of people at a baseball game, riders waiting for a train at a busy subway station, shoppers in a department store at Christmas time, and skiers on a slope in the middle of winter.

Crowds can be expressive or acting. They can be further subdivided into mobs, audiences, riots, and panics.

Expressive Crowds

An expressive crowd is one that desires to express the feelings shared by its members but releases these feelings in a fairly contained manner. Such crowds stimulate their members. Spectators at a basketball game and participants at a political rally are examples of expressive crowds.

Acting Crowds

An acting crowd aims its actions at a particular target or individual, with a primary goal of bringing about some sort of change. Its members are often upset and have a keen desire to take some sort of action that will help their cause. Examples of acting crowds include demonstrators, a lynch mob, and persons participating in a riot.

Mobs

Mob behavior generally results when resentment, frustration, and anxiety have been building up over a long period of time. A mob usually forms with the onset of a specific event, one that evokes intense feelings of anger and hostility. A mob may be either an acting crowd or an expressive crowd. It is expressive if its members merely behave in unison, acting if its members are ready to engage in behavior directed at some individual or institution. Collectivities that are engaged in vandalism, destruction of property, violence, sit-ins, or the taking over of a building are all examples of acting mobs. The objectives of these mobs may be to create better living conditions, settle an account with an individual or group who has harmed them, or get fair treatment by employers, the police, or the government.

Audiences

An audience is a crowd whose interest is centered on events and persons external to the collectivity itself. The audience is apt to act in a passive or receptive way. The level of communication between members of the audience is extremely limited, but between the stimulus and each member it may be great.

Riots

A violent and aggressive crowd that destroys property or causes people to be injured is labeled a riot.

Panics

A panic develops when a crowd collectively becomes hysterical because of a commonly shared belief. The panic is characterized by fear, confusion, and an absence of effective leadership. This type of collective behavior usually results because of some stress-producing crisis, particularly one of danger in which escape is in question.

Mass Behavior

In the definition of crowd behavior, the physical proximity of a group of individuals influences the behavior of that group. Individuals can also be influenced by the actions of others they never meet or interact with directly. In this sense, mass behavior is another form of collective behavior. It is not the action of individuals as a collectivity, but the aggregate actions of individuals. It includes rumor, fad or fashion, the craze, mass hysteria, the public, and public opinion.

Rumor

A rumor is a message that is widely passed among individuals. It is unverified at the moment and may or may not ultimately be supported by fact. When individuals are extremely anxious to get news about something but cannot secure any reliable information, they are prone to accepting rumors. Such rumors are most likely to spread if they support one's prejudices or justify one's beliefs. Rumors have provided most race riots with a major impetus, for misleading bits of information have often swept through crowds and encouraged violent and destructive behavior.

Fad or Fashion

Many people believe that they may gain status by behaving in a way that is different or novel. A fad is just such a change in behavior that takes place over a relatively short period of time. Fads grow quickly, reach their peak, and then rapidly decline. Examples of fads from the 1960s and 1970s include "streaking" and the use of certain catch phrases such as "oh, wow" and "far out."

Fashions, although similar to fads, represent customs that are only periodically subject to change. Change through fashions is not nearly so radical and rapid as is change through fads. Fashions are more typically reflected in one's style of dress, the length of one's hair, or some other aspect of appearance.

Craze

A craze is an unconventional pattern of behavior that a relatively small number of persons are obsessed with over a short period of time. The larger population often regards the craze as being somewhat unusual. Examples of crazes include flag-pole sitting, religious revivals, hula hoops, and political bandwagons.

Mass Hysteria

When individuals lose their self-control and behave in emotional or irrational ways, they may be experiencing mass hysteria. Because a rational course of action cannot be undertaken, people panic and thus reinforce each others' irrational behavior. Thus, panics and mass hysteria are related forms of collective behavior. When panics occur, people are overwhelmed by fear, which in turn causes them to react in emotional or irrational ways. Mass hysteria is a description of the reaction that a collectivity displays after its members have panicked. On October 30, 1938, Orson Welles presented "The War of the Worlds," a radio play. The broadcast was so realistic that hundreds of thousands of radio listeners around the country believed that Martians were landing in New Jersey and the United States was under attack. As a result of this broadcast, mass hysteria erupted in some areas.

Public

The public is a category of individuals who are not together physically but who are concerned about a particular issue, such as juvenile delinquency, prostitution, deterioration of urban neighborhoods, integration in the schools, the draft, gangs, taxation, or consumer rights. Because they believe the issue has considerable importance, members of the public communicate with one another in an attempt to resolve the issue and influence public opinion. A public may make its feelings known to the larger society through the mass media and other channels.

Public Opinion and Propaganda

Propaganda is the presentation of information for the purpose of manipulating public opinion toward a specific point of view. Information is presented with the purpose of influencing people to revise their values or beliefs in a particular way. Propaganda appeals to peoples' emotions because it is concerned with issues about which they are anxious or worried. Nearly all self-interest groups develop propaganda that will support their particular cause.

Propaganda is most effective when it deals with issues of immediate concern and when it is consistent with a person's values, sentiments, and beliefs. Its effectiveness is limited when there are competing propagandas, when the credibility of the propagandist is subject to question, or when the receiver of the propaganda has access to more reliable sources of information.

Social Movements

A social movement is a collective effort by a group of individuals to modify or maintain some element of the larger society. Social movements differ from the elementary forms of collective behavior (such as a mob) in that they are more tightly organized and have a life span that is considerably longer. Furthermore, the social movement has officially designated leaders, while the more elementary forms of collective behavior do not. The primary difference between the social movement and the institution is the permanence of the institution compared to the temporary nature of the social movement. The social movement becomes institutionalized when it has been accepted by the members of society. However, if society does not accept it, the social movement may disintegrate or die. Examples of social movements include the civil rights movement, the women's liberation movement, and the gay and lesbian rights movement.

Characteristics of Social Movements

All social movements have three characteristics: (1) goals, (2) a planned course of action for reaching those goals, and (3) an ideology or philosophy that justifies their existence. A social movement usually has a broad set of goals or objectives that are clearly established. A social movement directed at improving the lot of a given group will most likely identify as objectives several areas that must be changed if the movement is to be successful. The programs available for reaching these goals vary widely, ranging from nonviolent sit-ins to murder and the destruction of property. Finally, the ideology of a social movement is what brings its members together, for not only will the ideology provide a criticism of social conditions as they now exist, but in addition it will spell out the objectives of the movement and the methods that will be used to meet those objectives.

For example, the goal of the women's liberation movement is to end discrimination against women. The members of the movement plan to reach this goal by making all women aware that they are being discriminated against and attempting to persuade women to stop tolerating such treatment. The movement distributes literature, forms discussion groups, and makes certain that women have an active voice in government and business. Their members work to encourage the enactment of laws that will help their cause, and they fight to get women placed in influential positions in government. The movement justifies its actions by asserting that women have a right to expect to be treated fairly, to develop their talents, and to determine the course of their own existence.

Sociological Study of Social Movements

Sociologists study social movements in a number of ways: (1) by becoming actual participants in them and observing the actions of their members (participant observation research), (2) by gathering literature about them and interviewing participants, (3) by working with historical documents, and (4) by studying the membership rolls of a particular social movement in order to discover what types of people make up the movement's population.

Kinds of Social Movements

The values of the population of a society sometimes change as people are exposed to new ideas and other significant modifications that take place in their culture. These changes or modifications that gradually transform a culture are called *cultural drift*. As values change, many people become dissatisfied with their present lifestyle and attempt to bring about other changes in society that are consistent with their needs. The extent of the desired change and the type of change differ from one kind of social movement to another. Furthermore, some social movements try to prevent change from occurring in society. In the following paragraphs, several different types of social movements are discussed, namely: expressive movements, regressive (reactionary) movements, progressive movements, conservative movements, reform movements, revolutionary movements, utopian movements, and migratory movements.

Expressive Movements

When individuals believe that they are faced with a hopeless situation, an expressive movement may take place. Expressive movements do not try to bring about or forestall change; their aim is to help their members improve themselves or attain self-fulfillment. Individuals participating in an expressive movement modify their perception of an unpleasant external reality rather than change the external condition itself. For example, the Jehovah's Witness and Alcoholics Anonymous movements are geared toward helping their participants, not at making changes in society at large.

Regressive Movements

A regressive movement attempts to return conditions to a former state, to "turn back the clock." Individuals who join this type of movement are obviously unhappy with current social trends. The Ku Klux Klan is an example of a regressive movement. The major objectives of the KKK are to deny blacks their civil rights and liberties and return them to their low status of the past.

Progressive Movements

A progressive movement is one that attempts to improve society by making positive changes in its institutions and organizations. It advocates that society attempt new ways of doing things. The labor movement in the United States in the early twentieth century was a progressive movement.

Conservative Movements

A conservative movement tries to keep society from being changed. Individuals who support this type of movement see the present state of society as being the most desirable. The individuals who have organized themselves to stop passage of the equal rights amendment for women make up a conservative movement. In general, they believe that new legislation banning discrimination based on gender is unnecessary and may even be damaging to society.

Reform Movements

A reform movement is an attempt to modify some aspect of the society without completely transforming it. The gay and lesbian liberation movement is an example of a reform movement. The singular objective of this movement is to obtain equal rights and protection for gay and lesbian members of society without changing any other aspects of society.

Revolutionary Movements

A revolutionary movement is a movement that involves a quick and drastic change within society. The intent is to overthrow the existing social system and replace it with another. The New Left movement of the 1960s is an example of a revolutionary movement. The dominant group in the early years of this movement was the Students for a Democratic Society (SDS). By the end of the decade, SDS's aim was to quickly and drastically change the social order.

Utopian Movements

The utopian movement seeks to create an ideal social environment for a rather small group of followers. Utopian movements are sometimes also referred to as withdrawal or separatist movements. Individuals participating in these movements do not find the present society desirable. However, rather than attempting to change it, they withdraw by forming their own community either inside or outside the boundaries of the society, adopting a new lifestyle and behavior patterns. The self-sufficient rural commune, which was so popular in the United States during the 1960s, serves as an excellent example of a utopian movement.

Migratory Movements

Individuals who join a migratory movement have likely experienced much discontent with their present set of circumstances and have moved elsewhere with the hope of finding a brighter future. The migration to Israel by Jews throughout the world is an example of a migratory movement.

Development of a Social Movement

Not all social movements follow the same pattern of development. All movements, however, begin at a time of crisis, grow at various rates, and then either disappear or become institutionalized. Sociologists suggest that most social movements go through a pattern of development consisting of the following stages:

1. *Unrest Stage (Incipiency)*. During this stage, a general discontent is created by a malfunction of the system. Individuals are often dissatisfied and frustrated because they realize that they have been treated unjustly and recognize that they are unable to solve their problems individually. This stage may be rather extended, or the discontent may quickly lead to the next stage.

2. *Excitement Stage (Coalescence)*. After attention has been focused on the conditions causing unrest, a collectivity is gathered. The excitement present within the collectivity is generated by agitators or leaders. Leaders make individuals aware that they are not alone in experiencing unjust treatment. As individuals learn about the ways in which their problems can be solved, they become even more

excited. This excitement encourages them to unite, recruit others, maintain enthusiasm, and work together.

3. *Formalization Stage.* During this stage, a formal organized structure, with a hierarchy of officers, emerges. One of the more important functions of the formalization stage is to make the ideology of the movement clear to a membership that is now organized. The reasons for discontent, the plan of action, and the objectives of the movement are spelled out in detail.

4. *Institutionalization Stage.* If the movement is successful in attracting followers and winning the support of the public, institutionalization will eventually occur. During this stage, a bureaucracy is established and professional disciplined leadership replaces the charismatic figures of the earlier stages.

5. *Dissolution Stage.* If the movement does not become institutionalized because of internal conflicts, it may fragment and dissolve.

Successful Social Movements

Many movements are characterized by riots, violence, and demonstrations. These behaviors are detrimental to society when they injure others or destroy property. However, they may also help to bring about needed social change. Successful movements have resulted in the institutionalization of programs that have ensured the equal protection and equal rights of many groups who at one time were discriminated against. Furthermore, successful movements have led to changes in legislation that have produced a new and better life for millions of people.

The success of a movement is dependent on several conditions: the dedication and loyalty of its members, the presence of an effective leader, and the social conditions conducive to bringing people together.

Loyalty of Members

For a movement to be successful, it must have the support and loyalty of its members. This support is gathered and maintained in most instances through the use of propaganda, speeches, slogans, badges, and ideologies. The civil rights movement produced its share of propaganda, charismatic leaders who made emotional speeches (Malcolm X), slogans ("Black is beautiful"), and ideology (abolition of the separate-but-equal doctrine in education).

Leadership

No movement can be successful without an effective leader. A leader of a social movement must (1) have the ability to recruit and rally masses of people in support of the goals and objectives of the movement and (2) to maintain a sense of cohesion within a movement, making members constantly aware of their shared values and goals.

Charismatic Leaders

A charismatic leader of a social movement is particularly success-ful in inspiring enthusiasm among followers, arousing excitement, and encouraging them to unite. He/she may be a member of the group attempting to promote change or may be a member of a more privileged class. Charismatic leaders in the civil rights movements included such individuals as Malcolm X and Martin Luther King.

Administrative Leaders

The role of an administrative leader is very different from that of a charismatic leader. The administrative leader must be concerned with very practical matters, including the organization of the movement, the delegation of duties and responsibilities, recruitment, fund-raising, and public relations. Whitney Young is an example of an administrative leader.

Conducive Social Conditions

Social movements tend to be successful when certain conditions present within a society serve to bring people together into a collec-tivity. Conditions such as widespread discontent, frustration, social disorganization, insecurity, anomie, and alienation all will move people to search for a better life. When the above conditions are accompanied by a perceived social injustice, the motivation for joining a social movement is even more intense. Those individuals who joined the gay and lesbian rights movement were discontented with and frustrated by the fact that they had to hide their sexual orientation. They were often insecure when dealing with others for fear that their sexual preference would be discovered and that they would lose jobs, apartments, and friends. They joined the movement to find remedies to these problems.

Glossary

Acculturation A display of acceptance and adoption of the dominant culture by the minority group.

Achieved status Status acquired through hard work and demonstrated ability.

Acting crowd A crowd whose actions are aimed at a particular target or individual. The primary purpose of the acting crowd is to bring about change.

Age-specific rates The birth rate or death rate for specific age levels in the population.

Amalgamation Intermarriage between different racial groups, thereby producing a new stock of individuals.

Annihilation The process whereby members of a minority group are deliberately murdered by the dominant group.

Anomie A state of normlessness or rootlessness that results when cultural expectations are inconsistent with social realities.

Antinatal policies Governmental policies in favor of increasing the birth rate.

Applied sociology The search for knowledge to be used in practical ways.

Archaeology The scientific study of the material remains of extinct civilizations.

Ascribed status Status acquired by the individual at birth.

Assimilation The merging of two different cultures into a single culture containing characteristics of both.

Audience A group of people whose interest is centered on an outside stimulus.

Authoritarian leader Leader who makes all group decisions on his/her own.

Bureaucracy The mechanism that is used by formal organizations in order to reach its goals; a bureaucracy is a hierarchical authority structure and operates under predetermined rules and regulations.

Case study Maintenance of a complete and comprehensive record of all details related to a subject under study.

Caste A rigid system of social stratification that locks people into a particular layer of the social strata.

Classical conditioning Learning in which a previously neutral stimulus is paired with a response-producing stimulus until the neutral stimulus elicits the response.

Closed society A society in which an individual is locked into a given social class.

Codes of behavior Formal rules of conduct and informal traditions appropriate to certain roles.

Coefficient of correlation Measurement of the relationship existing between two or more set of variables.

Cohort A group of people who are socialized during the same period of time.

Collective behavior Noninstitutionalized, unstructured, spontaneous, emotional, and unpredictable patterns of group behavior.

Collectivity A group that engages in collective behavior.

Community A specific group of people who reside in a distinct geographical area, share a common culture, and are capable of acting collectively toward a given goal.

Concentric zone theory A theory which hypothesizes that cities grow in circular zones, spreading outward from the center.

Conflict perspective A theoretical perspective that views society as consisting of different groups and classes that have conflicts of interest.

Conservative movement A movement that attempts to keep society from being changed.

Control group Subjects in an experiment whose responses are compared with those who are subjected to the independent variable.

Convenience sample In data-gathering, a sample that contains individuals who are readily available to the researcher.

Counterculture   A group that challenges and rejects the norms and expectations of the dominant culture.

Craze   A nonconventional pattern of behavior with which a relatively small number of people are obsessed over a short period of time.

Crescive change   Changes that are unplanned and take place through the natural course of events.

Cross-sectional study   A comparison of situations existing among different groups at the same point in time.

Crowd   A gathering of people who are in close physical proximity to one another.

Crude birthrate   The number of births per year, per each 1,000 people in the population.

Crude death date   The number of deaths per year, per each 1,000 people in the population.

Cultural (social) anthropology   The scientific study of the ways of life among communities throughout the world.

Cultural change   Changes that take place in the culture of a people.

Cultural drift   A broad and gradual change in the values or behavior of a population.

Cultural integration   The functional, integrated organization of all traits and complexes in a culture.

Cultural lag   The time gap between a change in the material culture and the corresponding changes in the relevant nonmaterial culture.

Cultural norm   An established standard of what should exist within a particular culture.

Cultural pluralism   A form of accommodation in which different racial or ethnic groups live together, each maintaining its own customs.

Cultural relativity   A concept which holds that the meaning and value of a trait must be judged in relation to the trait's cultural context if it is to be fully understood.

Cultural symbol   Identifying signs that are used to serve as reminders of the presence of an institution.

Culture   The sum total of all learned behavioral traits, values, beliefs, language, laws, and technology characteristic of the members of a society.

Culture complex A cluster of related traits.

Culture trait The smallest unit of a culture.

Democratic leader A leader who looks to the group for ideas and proposals in order to make decisions and attain group goals.

Demography The systematic study of population.

Dependent variable The outcome variable that the researcher is interested in measuring.

Deviance Any behavior that fails to conform to the expectations of society or a given group in society.

Diffusion The introduction of a new trait from an external culture.

Discovery Knowledge that already exists in a culture but is finally verified and put to use.

Discrimination An overt behavior pattern that is directed toward a minority group.

Ecology The study of the interrelationship of organisms and the physical environment.

Economics The study of the production, distribution, and consumption of goods and services.

Ecosystem The interrelationship of all life forms that inhabit the environment.

Ectomorph A body type identified by W. H. Sheldon as skinny, bony, and fragile.

Ego The conscious, rational part of the self

Enacted change Changes that are intentionally planned and executed.

Enacted role The way in which a person actually carries out a role.

Encounter group Any one of a variety of sensitivity groups whose members meet for meditation or consciousness-expansion.

Endogamy A cultural norm which dictates that a person must marry within a specified group.

Endomorph A body type identified by Sheldon as round, soft, and fat.

Ethnic group A group of individuals who share certain cultural characteristics such as language, religion, and nationality.

Ethnocentrism The tendency of individuals in a society to assume the superiority of their own culture.

Exogamy A cultural norm which dictates that a person must marry outside a specified group.

Experiment A study in which all variables except the one under investigation are held constant. This variable (the independent variable) is then manipulated to see what results will follow.

Ex post facto study Researching a situation that has already occurred, often by using recorded data.

Expressive crowd A crowd that expresses the feelings shared by its members in a fairly contained manner.

Expressive movement An attempt by individuals to modify their perception of an unpleasant external reality rather than change the external condition itself.

Expulsion The forceful eviction of a minority group from a territory.

Extended family The nuclear family plus other important relatives such as grandparents, uncles, and aunts.

External validity The extent to which results from the subject(s) in the present study can be generalized to individual(s) not presently under investigation.

Fad A change in behavior that takes place over a relatively short period of time, grows quickly, peaks, and then rapidly declines.

Fashion Customs that are periodically subject to change.

Fecundity The biological capacity of women to reproduce.

Fertility The rate of reproduction in a society.

Folkways Customary, habitual ways of acting within a society.

Formal organization A group of individuals who, in coordinating their activities, follow an explicitly stated set of rules and regulations for the purpose of achieving a specific goal.

Formal structure A large association of people deliberately organized to follow specific rules in order to achieve given objectives.

Frequency How often a specific phenomenon occurs.

Functionalist perspective A theoretical perspective that views society as an integrated whole. All parts of the society perform certain functions for the needs of a stable and consensual society.

Gemeinschaft A term used to describe a community in which most relationships are intimate, personal, and traditional.

Gender identity One's concept of self as being masculine or feminine.

Gender roles Socially constructed behavioral expectations for males and females.

Generalized other A composite of the collective expectations that an individual believes others hold toward him or her.

Geography The study of the role of the features of the earth and their effect on the growth, decline, and movement of world populations.

Gesellschaft A term used to describe a society based on impersonal relationships and a lack of commitment to traditional ties.

Group A number of people interacting together who share a consciousness of membership based on shared expectations of behavior.

Group marriage A form of marriage in which two or more men are living with two or more women at the same time.

History The recording and explanation of past events in terms of human activities.

Horizontal mobility Social movement from one position to another on the same social plane.

Hypothesis A tentative theoretical statement relating all known facts.

Id In Freud's theory of personality, the most primitive or instinctive part of personality, operating according to the pleasure principle.

Ideology A system of interdependent ideas that is shared by a group and that justifies the interests of its members.

Incest taboo The prohibition of sexual relations between blood-related family members.

Incidence How many of a specific phenomenon.

Independent variable A variable that is manipulated within the study.

Informal structure A group of people who do not operate according to rules and regulations and have the flexibility for change.

In-group A group of persons with whom the individual feels comfortable and has a sense of belonging.

Institution An organized, patterned system of social relationships that exists to meet the needs of the group.

Institutionalization The development of a regular system of circumscribed norms, statuses, and roles that are accepted by society.

Integration A social arrangement in which both dominant and minority groups live together in harmony.

Intergenerational mobility Social mobility that takes place between generations.

Internal migration The movement of people from one region of a country to another.

Internal validity The extent to which the data obtained actually reflect the real condition(s) of the subject(s) under investigation.

Internalization An aspect of the socialization process in which an individual incorporates the norms of a culture and conforms to those norms.

International migration The movement of people from one country to another.

Intragenerational mobility Social mobility that takes place within the same generation.

Invention The creation of something new by combining two or more elements that already exist within a culture.

Involuntary group Those groups in which individuals are placed, through no choice of their own.

Kinesics A type of nonverbal behavior involving body movements, such as hand movements or facial expressions.

Kinship A large network of people who are related to one another.

Laissez-faire leader A leader who promotes a "hands off" approach to directing group activities and goals.

Latent functions Functions of a social institution that are not obvious and apparent to the members of a society.

Laws Mores that have been formalized and have legal sanctions attached to them.

Life expectancy The number of years that the average infant may expect to live.

Life span   The length of life that is possible for a given species.

Linguistics   The study of the structure of language and how it affects our ways of thinking and perceiving.

Longitudinal study   Study and observation carried out over an extended period of time.

Looking-glass self   The mirror-image reflection of the self provided by the reaction of others to one's behavior.

Manifest functions   Functions of a social institution that are obvious, apparent, and generally accepted by the members of society.

Mass hysteria   The behavior that results when groups of individuals lose their self-control and behave in emotional or irrational ways.

Matched-pair technique   Selection of subjects for a control group who match corresponding subjects in the experimental group.

Mean   The arithmetic average.

Median   The number that falls midway in a distribution of numbers.

Mere exposure effect   An effect in which continual interaction with another person breeds familiarity and produces positive attitudes toward that person.

Mesomorph   A body type identified by W. H. Sheldon as muscular or athletic.

Migration   The movement of people from one geographical location to another.

Migratory movement   A movement in which individuals leave their present society in an attempt to find a better life for themselves elsewhere.

Minority group   A category of individuals who are distinguished from a larger population of which they are a part.

Mob   An acting crowd that is emotionally aroused.

Mode   The number that appears most often in a distribution of numbers.

Monogamy   A marriage of one woman and one man.

Mores   The more important folkways carrying significant implications of right or wrong, good or bad.

Multiple-nuclei theory   A theory which hypothesizes that cities grow in no specific pattern. Cities have specialized areas of which each represents a nucleus, and each nucleus influences growth and development in the surrounding area.

Negative sanctions The punishments that may be applied when an individual fails to conform to the expectations of a group or society.

Nonparticipant observation A method of sociological study in which a researcher observers a group or setting without interacting or participating in the phenomenon under investigation.

Nuclear family A family unit consisting of the husband, wife, and their children; sometimes referred to as "conjugal" family.

Observational study A study in which the researcher records his/her systematic observations of an actual rather than an arranged situation.

Oligarchy Rule by a few individuals who occupy the highest positions in the organization.

Open society A society that affords an individual the opportunity to move upward to a higher or lower social class.

Operant conditioning Learning in which the consequences of behavior determine whether or not it will be repeated.

Opportunity structure An individual has the opportunity to participate in a role.

Out-group A group to which an individual does not belong.

Panic The behavior that develops when a crowd becomes hysterical.

Paralanguage A type of nonverbal vocal behavior, such as pitch or loudness of speech.

Participant observation A method of sociological study in which a researcher participates in the group or setting that is being studied.

Physical anthropology The study of human evolution.

Political science The study of government, political philosophy, and public administrative decision making.

Polyandry Marriage of one woman to more than one man.

Polygamy Marriage of a person of either sex to more than one spouse.

Polygyny Marriage of one man to more than one woman.

Positive sanctions Those rewards that are given to an individual who conforms to the expectations of the group or society.

Prejudice A prejudging attitude or feeling that a person has toward members of a minority group.

Prescribed norm A norm that specifies something that an individual should do.

Prescribed role The manner in which society expects individuals to carry out a particular role.

Primary deviance Deviant behavior that is temporary and confined to only a small part of a person's life.

Primary group A small group in which interaction among people is intimate and personal.

Progressive movement A movement that attempts to improve society by making positive changes in its institutions and organizations.

Pronatal policies Governmental policies oriented toward limiting population growth.

Propaganda The presentation of actual or alleged facts for the purpose of manipulating public opinion toward a specific point of view.

Proscribed norm A norm that specifies something that an individual must not do.

Prospective study A study beginning with the present and extending into the future.

Proxemics A type of nonverbal behavior involving interpersonal spacing or body postures.

Psychology The study of individual behavior and processes.

Public A category of physically separated individuals who share a common concern in a public matter.

Race A category of individuals who through generations of inbreeding share certain biological or physical characteristics.

Racism The belief that the racial group to which one belongs is superior to other racial groups.

Random sample In data-gathering, a sample in which every individual in the group (or population) has an equally likely chance of being selected into the sample.

Random-assignment technique Placing of subjects in either the control group or the experimental group by using statistically random assignments.

Range The interval containing the numbers in the distribution.

Reference group A group that serves as a model when making evaluations and judgments about oneself.

Reform movement A movement that attempts to modify some aspect of the society without completely transforming it.

Regressive movement A movement that attempts to return conditions to a former state.

Reliability The extent to which the same research method will produce the same results each time the method is employed.

Research design An outline of what is to be studied, processed, and analyzed in a scientific experiment.

Revolutionary movement A movement that attempts to completely overthrow the existing social system and replace it with another.

Riot The result of the actions of a violent and aggressive crowd.

Role Behavior expected of those who occupy a given status.

Role conflict A condition produced when an individual holds one or more statuses that require contradictory role expectations.

Role distance A characteristic in which an individual carries out a role in an emotionally detached manner.

Role identity The self concept of ourselves as we are enacting a specific role.

Role strain A condition that exists when an individual has difficulty in carrying out the expectations of a role because of ambiguous obligations.

Role-taking The acting out of the behavior of a role that one does not hold.

Rumor A message that is passed among individuals but is not supported by fact.

Sanctions A system of rewards and punishments developed by a society.

Secondary deviance Deviant behavior of a rather serious nature, in which the individual's deviance plays a major role in his/her life and the person is publicly identified as a deviant.

Secondary group A group in which interaction among members is impersonal, utilitarian, and specific.

Sector theory A theory which hypothesizes that cities grow from their in center in wedge-shaped sectors, according to their transportation routes.

Segregation The practice of forcing members of the less powerful group to establish residences and facilities apart from the dominant group.

Self ("the self") A view of oneself as a distinct, separate entity with a personal identity that others respond to.

Self-segregation The process whereby members of the minority group voluntarily separate themselves from the rest of society.

Separatism The establishment of a new society by the minority group.

Sex ratio The number of males per each 1000 females in a given population.

Sexual identity The concept of self one has based on one's sexual orientation.

Sexuality The feelings and drives as well as the sexual practices common to a society.

Significant other A person who exercises a major influence over the attitudes and behavior of an individual.

Social change A change or alteration in the social structure of a society, usually occurring over a period of time.

Social class A stratum of persons who share the same position in the social-status continuum.

Social control All means and methods used to induce a person to conform to the expectations of a group or society.

Social distance A measurement of the degree of closeness or acceptance one has toward members of other groups.

Social mobility The movement of an individual or group from one social status to another.

Social movement A collective effort by a group of individuals to modify or maintain an element of the larger society.

Social psychology The study of the individual's relationship with a group.

Social status The social position that an individual holds in a group.

Social stratification A ranking of individuals in accordance with the number of desirable qualities they possess.

Socialization The process of social interaction through which an individual internalizes the way of life of his/her society and attaches meaning to the social life around him/her.

Society A group of people who live together over an extended period, occupy a territory, and eventually begin to organize themselves into a social unit distinct from other groups.

Sociobiology The study of the biological basis of social behavior.

Socio-emotional leader A leader who creates feelings of good will and harmony in the group.

Sociology The scientific study of the group life of human beings and the resulting social behavior.

Spoken language A set of sounds with meanings attached that is shared by members of the group.

Standardized birth rates and death rates Adjusted rates that take into account differences between populations by considering certain vital characteristics that may affect birthrate or death rate.

Status The social position held by an individual in a group or by a group in society.

Status inconsistency A condition in which an individual holds a number of different statuses at the same time and the statuses are incompatible with one another.

Stereotypes Generalized preconceived beliefs about how all the individuals in a certain religious, racial, or ethnic category will think and act.

Subculture A set of behavior patterns that are similar to those of the dominant culture yet distinguishable from them, too.

Superego The part of the self that has absorbed the cultural values; the conscience.

Survey A study using a proportion of a large group (or population). Data are collected using a questionnaire or an interview.

Symbolic communication An exchange of information through verbal, non-verbal and written language that has an agreed-upon meaning to the members of the group.

Task leader A leader who organizes and directs the group toward the group goals.

Therapeutic group A group in which members share a common problem, addiction, or issue and unite for social support.

Urbanization The process that occurs when large numbers of people leave the rural regions of the country and establish urban residence.

Utopian movement A movement that attempts to create an ideal society for a small group of followers.

Validity The extent to which data obtained actually reflect the real conditions.

Values Deep-seated sentiments shared by members of a society.

Vertical mobility A change in status for the individual either up or down on the social class hierarchy.

Voluntary group Those groups of which an individual chooses to become a member.

Volunteer sample In data-gathering, a sample in which every individual in the sample has volunteered to participate in the study.

Written language The graphic recording of spoken language.

INDEX

A

Acculturation, 137
Achieved status, 42
Administrative leaders, 178
Age-specific rate, 153-154
Amalgamation, 135
American Journal of Sociology, 9
American Sociological Association (ASA), 9
American Sociological Society, 9
Annihilation, 134-135
Anomie, 67-70
Anonymity, 167
Anti-Defamation League (ADL), 138
Antinatal policies, 157-158
Ascribed status, 42
Assimilation, 135
Audiences, 170
Authoritarian leaders, 83

B

Bem, Sandra L., 55
Birthrates, 154
Blended family, 101
Bureaucracy, 93-98
Bureaucratic personality, 97
Burgess, Ernest, 161

C

Case studies, 12-13
Charismatic leaders, 178
Children:
    care and protection of, 102
    socialization of, 103
Class, 119-125
Classical conditioning, in sexuality, 49-50
Closed societies, 127-128
Coalescence, 176-177
Coefficient of correlation, 22-23
Cohabitation, 101-102
Cohort changes, 149
Collective behavior, 153-172
    and crowd behavior, 169-170
    determinants of, 164-166
    and mass behavior, 170-172
    theories of, 166-168
Collectivity, 164
Comte, Auguste, 8
    theory of social change, 144-145
Concentric zone theory, 161
Confidentiality, in research techniques, 24-25
Conflict theory:
    in deviant behavior, 71
    of social change, 146
Conservative movements, 175

Contagion theory of collective behavior, 166-168
Control groups, 14-15
Control theory, 69-70
Convenience sample, 19
Convergence theory of collective behavior, 168
Cooley, Charles Horton, 40-41
Countercultures, 33-34
Craze, 171
Cresive change, 139
Cross-sectional studies, 20-21
Crowd behavior, 169-170
Crude birthrate, 153
Crude death rate, 153
Cultural change (see Social change)
Cultural complexes and institutions, 33
Cultural drift, 174
Cultural pluralism, 136
Cultural traits, 32
Culture:
  change and lag in, 36
  ethnocentrism, 34-35
  norms of, 31-32
  organization of, 32-34
  and society, 29-30
  symbolic communication, 30-31
Cyclical theories, 145-146

D

Data-gathering techniques, 18-19
Death rates, 154
Democratic leaders, 83
Demographic transition theory, 156-157
Demography (see Population)
Deviance, 61-72
  anomie theory, 67-68
  biological explanations, 63-65
  body-type theories, 64-65
  chromosome theories, 65
  comparison of theories, 69-72
  conflict theory, 71
  control theory, 69
  deviant behavior, 61-63
  deviant subcultures, 63
  differential association theory, 66-67
  explanations of, 63-72

Deviance (cont.)
  group deviation, 62
  individual deviation, 62
  labeling theory, 70-71
  psychoanalytic theories, 65
  psychological explanations, 65
  sociological explanations, 66-72
  sociological relevance, 63
Deviant subcultures, 63
Differential association theory, 69-70
Diffusion, in social change, 146-147
Discrimination, 133-134
Divorce, 111-114
Double standard, 52-53
Dramatic role presentation, 45-46
Durkheim, Emile, 8
Dynamic Sociology (L. Ward), 8

E

Ecology, 158
Economics, and social institutions, 90
Ecosystem, 158
Education:
  and social institutions, 89-90
  and social mobility, 128-129
Ego, 48
Elderly, care and protection of, 102
Emergent norm theory, 168
Encounter groups, 80
Endogamy, 106
Essay on the Principles of Population (T. Malthus), 156
Ethnic groups:
  basic concepts of, 132
  changing relations with racial groups, 138-139
Ethnic relations, 131-139
Ethnocentrism, 34-35
  basic concepts of, 133
Ex-post facto studies, 21
Exogamy, 106
Experimental studies, 15-16
Expressive movements, 174
Extended family, 100-101

F

Fad or fashion, 171
Family:
  cohabitation, 101-102
  extended, 100-101
  functions of, 89, 102-104
  influence on mate selection, 106
  kinship, 102, 109
  loss of economic and protective func-
      tions, 110-111
  loss of socialization function, 110
  nuclear, 100
  protective function, 102
  reconstituted (or blended), 101
  role changes, 112
  single-parent, 101
  as a socialization agent, 38-39, 103
  sociology and, 307
  structure changes, 111-112
  types of, 100-102
  weakening of extended kinship ties,
      109-110
Family background, 129
Fecundity, 154
Fertility, 154
Folkways, 31-32
Formal organizations:
  bureaucracy and, 93-98
  and social institutions, 84-98
Freud, Sigmund, 48-49
Functionalism, 52

G

Gemeinschaft, 79
Gender, and social mobility, 129-130
Gender roles, 54-56
Generalized belief, 165
Generalized other, 41
Genocide, 135
Gesellschaft, 79
Glueck, Eleanor, 64
Glueck, Sheldon, 64
Goal displacement, 97
Goring, Charles, 64
Government, 90
Group boundaries, 77

Group deviation, 62
Group marriage, 105
Group structure, 81-83
Groups (*see* Social groups)

H

Hierarchy of authority, 94-95
Hirschi, Travis, 69
Hollingshead, August, 122
Hoyt, Homer, 161-162

I

Id, 48
Impersonality:
  and bureaucracy, 95
  and collective behavior, 167
In-groups, 77-78
Incest taboo, 103-104, 106-107
Industrialization:
  effect on family, 109-112
  and social mobility, 128
Infirm, care and protection of, in the
    family, 102
Institutionalization, 87, 177
Institutions (*see* Social institutions)
Integrated cultures, 34
Integration of minority groups, 136
Involuntary groups, 76-77

K

Kinship, 102, 109

L

Labeling theory, 71-72
Laissez-faire leaders, 83
Language, 30
Laws, 32
Leadership:
  in social change, 148
  in social movements, 178
  styles of, 83
  types of, 82-83
Learning structure, 68
Libido, 48

Life expectancy, 154
Life span, 154
Lifestyles, 125
Lombroso, Cesare, 64
Longitudinal studies, 21
Looking-glass self, 40-41
Lower class, 124-125
Lower-middle class, 124
Lower-upper class, 123

M

Malthus, Thomas, 156
Marriage, 99-114
    endogamy, 106
    exogamy, 106
    group marriage, 105
    incest and, 106-107
    mate selection, 105-109
    monogamy, 104-105
    polygamy, 105
    social context, 107
    sociology and, 99-114
Marx, Karl, 8, 121
    theory of social change, 144-145
Mass behavior, 170-172
Mass hysteria, 171
Mass media, 40
Mate selection:
    influences of family and peers, 106
    interpersonal factors in, 107-108
    limiting rules of society, 106-107
    physical attractiveness, 107-108
    romantic love, 108
    similarity, 108
    theories of, 108-109
Mead, George Herbert, 41, 51
Mean, 22
Median, 22
Merton, Robert K., 67-68
Middle class, 123-124
Migration, 155
Migratory movements, 176
Minority groups, 132-138
    acculturaion of, 137
    Anti-Defamation League (ADL), 138
    assimilation and amalgamation of, 135
    basic concepts of, 132

Minority groups (*cont.*)
    coexistence of, 135-136
    creation of organizations, 138
    cultural pluralism of, 136
    expulsion and annihilation of, 134-135
    integration of, 136
    National Association for the
        Advancement of Colored People
        (NAACP), 138
    reactions to discrimination, 136-138
    segregation of, 136
    self-segregation of, 137
    separatism of, 137-138
Mobility (*see* Social mobility)
Mobilization for action, 166
Mobs, 169-170
Mode, 22
Monogamy, 104-105
Mores, 32
Multiple nuclei theory, 162

N

National Association for the
        Advancement of Colored
        People (NAACP), 138
Nonverbal behavior, 31
Nuclear family, 100

O

Observational methods, 16-17
Oligarchy, 96-97
Open societies, 127
Operant conditioning, in sexuality, 50
Opportunity structure, 68
Out-groups, 77-78

P

Peer groups, 39-40
Peers, influence in mate selection, 106
Personality, components of, 48
Polyandry, 105
Polygamy, 105
Polygyny, 105
Population, 152-158
    age-specific rate, 153-154

Population (*cont.*)
  antinatal policies, 157-158
  crude birthrate, 153
  crude death rate, 153
  demographic concepts, 153-154
  demographic transition theory,
    156-157
  demographic variables, 153
  fecundity, 154
  fertility, 154
  growth measurement, 154-155
  life expectancy, 154
  life span, 154
  Malthusian theory, 156
  migration and, 155
  optimum population, 154
  pronatal policies, 157
  sex ratio, 154
  and social change, 148-149
  technology and population growth,
    155-156
Prejudice, 133-134
Primary groups, 78
Professional ethics, 97-98
Progressive movements, 175
Pronatal policies, 157
Propaganda, 172-173
Prospective studies, 21-22
Psychosexual stages, 49
Public opinion, 172-173

R

Race, basic concepts of, 132
Racial groups, 138-139
Racism, 133
Random sample, 20
Range, 22
Reconstituted (or blended) family, 101
Reference groups, 78
Reform movements, 175
Regressive movements, 174-175
Reiss, Ira, 52-53
Reliability, 12
Religion, 90
Research techniques, 11-26
  case studies, 12-13

Research techniques (*cont.*)
  changing conditions in, 23-24
  ethical considerations, 24-25
  experiments, 13-16
  observational methods, 16-17
  reliability and validity, 12
  sociologist's role in, 25-26
  special issues in, 23-25
  statistics in, 22-23
  survey studies in, 17-20
  time factors involved in, 20-21
Retrospective studies, 21
Revolutionary movements, 175
Riots, 170
Ritualism:
  and bureaucracy, 97
  R. Merton's theory of deviant
    behavior, 67-68
Role, 43-46
Role conflict, 45
Role distance, 44
Role identity, 44
Role strain, 45
Rules of Sociological Method
    (E. Durkheim), 8
Rumor, 170-171
Rural communities, 159

S

Samples, types of, 19-20
School, as a socialization agent, 39
Scientific method, 6-7
Secondary groups, 79
Sector theory, in urbanization, 161-162
Segregation, 136
Self:
  development of, 40-46
  dramatic role presentation, 45-46
  and the generalized other, 41
  looking-glass self, 40-41
  reference groups and, 43-44
  role characteristics, 44-46
  and significant others, 41-42
  socialization and, 37-46
  and status, 42-43
Self-segregation, 137

Separatism, 137-138
Sex ratio, 154
Sexual activities, regulation in the
       family, 103-104
Sexual orientation, 56
Sexuality:
    attitudes and behaviors, 52-53
    classical conditioning and, 49-50
    education, 53-54
    functionalism, 52
    gender roles and, 54-56
    learning approaches, 49-50
    operant conditioning, 50
    psychoanalytic approach and, 48-49
    psychosexual stages of, 49
    social learning approach, 59
    sociobiological approach and, 48
    sociological approaches, 50-52
    symbolic interactionism, 51-52
    theoretical perspectives on, 47-52
Sheldon, William, 64
Smelser, Neil J., 164-165
Social change, 143-151
    agents of, 146-147
    definition of, 143-144
    rate factors of, 147-149
    resistance to, 149-150
    social planning, 150-151
    theories of, 144-146
Social class, 119-125
    life chances, 125
    lifestyles, 125
    lower class, 124-125
    middle class, 123-124
    social stratification and, 120-122
    in the United States, 123-125
    upper class, 123
    working class, 124
Social control, 57-72
    conflicting social norms, 59
    external social controls, 60-61
    internal social controls, 59-60
    sanctions in, 61
    social norms and, 58
Social distance, 77-78
Social groups, 75-83
    definition of, 75-76

Social groups (*cont.*)
    group structure, 81-83
    kinds of groups, 76-80
Social institutions, 84-93
    characteristics of, 85-86
    codes of behavior, 86-87
    competition among, 91-92
    cooperation among, 92
    cultural symbols, 86
    and economics, 90
    and education, 89-90
    and the family function, 89
    formal organizations, 93-98
    functions of, 88-92
    and government, 90
    ideology of, 87
    institutionalization, 87
    manifest and latent functions, 88-90
    organizational change and, 98
    relationships among, 90-92
    and religion, 90
    traits of, 86-87
    transfer of functions, 91
    universality and variation, 92-93
Social mobility, 125-130
    closed societies, 127-128
    definition of, 125
    education and, 128-129
    factors related to, 128-130
    family background and, 129
    gender and, 129-130
    horizontal mobility, 126
    industrialization and, 128
    intergenerational mobility, 126
    intragenerational mobility, 126-127
    open societies, 127
    types of, 126-127
    in the United States, 130
    vertical mobility, 126
Social movements, 172-179
    administrative leaders, 178
    characteristics of, 173
    charismatic leaders, 178
    conducive social conditions, 178-179
    conservative movements, 175
    development of, 176-177
    expressive movements, 174

Social movements (*cont.*)
  factors in success, 177-179
  kinds of, 174-176
  leadership, 178
  loyalty of members, 177-178
  migratory movements, 176
  progressive movements, 175
  reform movements, 175
  regressive movements, 174-175
  revolutionary movements, 175
  sociological study of, 173-174
  stages of, 174-175
  utopian movements, 175-176
Social norms, 58
Social planning, 150-151
Social stratification, 120-122
Socialization:
  agents of, 38-40
  goals of, 38
  and the self, 37-46
Socio-emotional leaders, 83
Sociobiology, 48
Sociologists, roles of, 25-26
Sociology:
  collective behavior, 153-172
  culture and, 29-36
  deviance and social control, 57-72
  ecology and, 158
  ethnic relations, 131-139
  historical development of, 7-9
  marriage and the family, 99-114
  and other sciences, 5
  population and, 152-158
  race and, 131-139
  research, 11-26
  as a science, 5-7
  scientific methods of investigation, 7
  sexuality and gender roles, 47-56
  social change, 143-151
  social class, 119-125
  social groups, 75-83
  social institutions and formal
    organizations, 84-98
  social mobility, 125-130
  social movements, 172-179
  socialization and the self, 37-46
  specialized fields in, 9-10

Sociology (*cont.*)
  the study of, 4-5
  urbanization and, 159-162
Spencer, Herbert, 8
  theory of social change, 144-145
Spoken language, 30
Statistics, 22-23
Status, 42-43
Status inconsistency, 43
Stereotypes, 133
Structural conduciveness, and collective
    behavior, 165
Structural strains, 165
Subcultures, 33
  deviant, 63
Suggestibility, 167-168
Superego, 48
Survey studies, 17-20
Symbolic communication, 30-31
Symbolic interactionism, 51

T

Task leaders, 83
Technology, 148
Thanatos, 48
Therapeutic groups, 80
Tonnies, Ferdinand, 79

U

Upper class, 123
Upper-middle class, 124
Upper-upper class, 123
Urban communities, and urbanization,
    59
Urban growth, patterns of, 161-162
Urban life, 160-161
Urbanization, 152-162
  convergene of rural and urban
    communities, 162
  factors contributing to, 159-160
  rural communities, 159
  urban communities, 159
Utopian movements, 175-176

V

Validity, 12

Values, cultural, 31
Variables, 14
Vertical mobility, 126
Voluntary groups, 76-77
Voluntary participation,
    in research techniques, 25
Volunteer sample, 19-20

W

Ward, Lester, 8
Warner, W. Lloyd, 122
Weber, Max, 8-9, 121
Working class, 124
Written language, 30-31

MADISON-JEFFERSON COUNTY PUBLIC LIBRARY

WITHDRAWN

301 COH 50214 8.95
Cohen, Bruce J., 1938-
INTRODUCTION TO
  SOCIOLOGY.

[OTHER BORROWERS WILL APPRECIATE]
  THE PROMPT RETURN OF THIS BOOK

MADISON-JEFFERSON COUNTY PUBLIC LIBRAR'